T0302407

REAL ESTATE INVESTING 101

FROM FINDING PROPERTIES AND **SECURING MORTGAGE TERMS** TO **REITs** AND **FLIPPING HOUSES,** AN ESSENTIAL PRIMER ON **HOW TO MAKE MONEY WITH REAL ESTATE**

MICHELE CAGAN, CPA

Adams Media
New York London Toronto Sydney New Delhi

Adams Media
An Imprint of Simon & Schuster, LLC
100 Technology Center Drive
Stoughton, MA 02072

First Adams Media hardcover edition June 2019

ADAMS MEDIA and colophon are trademarks of Simon & Schuster.

For information about special discounts for bulk purchases, please contact Simon & Schuster Special Sales at 1-866-506-1949 or business@simonandschuster.com.

The Simon & Schuster Speakers Bureau can bring authors to your live event. For more information or to book an event contact the Simon & Schuster Speakers Bureau at 1-866-248-3049 or visit our website at www.simonspeakers.com.

Manufactured in China

10 9 8 7 6 5 4 3 2 1

Library of Congress Cataloging-in-Publication Data
Names: Cagan, Michele, author.
Title: Real estate investing 101 / Michele Cagan, CPA.
Description: Avon, Massachusetts: Adams Media, 2019.
Series: Adams 101.
Includes index.
Identifiers: LCCN 2019006890 | ISBN 9781507210574 (hc) | ISBN 9781507210581 (ebook)
Subjects: LCSH: Real estate investment.
Classification: LCC HD1382.5 .C34 2019 | DDC 332.63/24--dc23
LC record available at https://lccn.loc.gov/2019006890

ISBN 978-1-5072-1057-4
ISBN 978-1-5072-1058-1 (ebook)

CONTENTS

INTRODUCTION

Compared to other types of investments, real estate ranks as one of the most profitable, least risky, and most stable choices (but if part of the fun for you is rollercoaster-like risk, there are real estate investments for you too). No matter what's going on in the world, people need a place to live and somewhere to work, and that means real estate will always be in demand, making it a perfect piece of every portfolio.

When you hear the phrase *real estate investing*, the first thing to come to your mind may be renting properties to tenants. Or you may think of house flipping, something becoming increasingly popular. It's true that these are types of real estate investing, but they're far from the only ones. Among the kinds of real estate investing to choose from are:

- Real estate mutual funds
- Real estate investment trusts (REITs)
- Exchange-traded funds (ETFs)
- Crowdfunded real estate

In this book, you'll learn about all these and more. You'll discover how to take advantage of special tax breaks, choose the most profitable properties, and even ways to start investing in real estate with as little as $50. With so many ways to get started, it's easier than ever to begin building your own real estate empire—a proven path to accumulating serious wealth without taking on bank-breaking risk.

Whether you're a novice in the art of real estate investing or you've had some experience and want to learn more, this book will be a reliable guide. You may want to become a full-time investor, flipping houses or managing properties. Or you may want to just dip your toes to make some money on the side. Either way, you need the advice offered in these pages.

Welcome to *Real Estate Investing 101*.

CHAPTER 1

THE WORLD OF REAL ESTATE INVESTING

Most people think of real estate investing as owning property to either rent out or flip. They're right, but real estate investing includes much more, from those physical money-making properties to real estate–related stocks to real estate investment clubs.

For people who prefer a hands-off approach, investing in real estate mutual funds, real estate investment trusts (REITs), and crowdfunded real estate provides the opportunity to reap rewards without the work and for much smaller investments. All it takes to get started is a little bit of money, some research, and a desire to build wealth.

WHAT REAL ESTATE IS

Land and Buildings

For most people the words *real estate* probably conjure up houses, but real estate is much more than that. There are dozens of types of real estate, and even more options when you turn to real estate investing. At the heart, though, real estate is made up of land and the buildings on it, as well as anything growing on the land or found underground (such as oil).

Unlike personal property, real property can't be moved, so its value is tied to its geography.

Who Owns America?

According to *The Washington Post*, 80 percent of Americans live on just 3 percent of the total available land in the United States. The federal government is the single biggest landowner, holding 28.7 percent. That's followed by the one hundred biggest private landowners, who together own about 40.2 million acres—nearly the size of New England.

RESIDENTIAL REAL ESTATE

Most people are familiar with residential real estate—it's where we all live. Residential real estate is controlled by zoning laws. These regulations define the number and types of homes that can be built in a specific area and may also control things like noise, pets, and whether business may be conducted from a home.

Underneath the residential umbrella, real estate is split into existing homes (also called resale homes) and new construction (never been lived in before). While single-family homes are the most common property in this category, they're still just one option out of many. Other types of residential real estate include:

- Condominiums: privately owned units within a larger structure that is collectively owned
- Cooperatives: where individuals own shares of the building and the right to live in their own units
- Townhomes: attached houses that may have condominium-style common areas
- Multi-family homes: which can hold anywhere from one to four individual units

The two ways to invest directly in residential real estate are renting property (a long-term investment) or flipping property (a short-term investment). You can also invest in these properties indirectly through real estate investment trusts (REITs) and crowdfunded residential rental properties.

You May Already Be a Real Estate Investor

If you own a home, whatever kind it is, you're already a real estate investor. For most homeowners, it's the biggest asset they have. As with other investment assets, you expect your home to increase in value over time; and given enough time, it will.

LAND

The most basic type of real estate is land, but even "land" encompasses more than just undeveloped vacant housing lots. In this category, you'll also find working land, which refers to properties such as:

- Farms
- Cattle ranches
- Timberland

Land also includes anything natural found on the property, such as trees, streams, oil, or minerals (for mining).

Unimproved Land

Raw, unimproved land refers to property that has no basic services. That means there's no gas, electricity, water, phone service, and sometimes even no roads.

This type of property may be very remote and hard to access. These parcels may also be found in rural areas, such as old farmland that hasn't yet been transformed to support housing or commercial buildings.

Use caution when buying unimproved properties. For one thing, it can be hard to obtain a clear title (proof of ownership). Also, if you are planning on developing the property, you need to make sure that you can get (or that there is) an easement (the right to use property in a certain way) that will let you bring utilities onto the land. And though they're usually pretty low, be aware that many state and local governments assess property taxes even on unimproved land.

In Development

Land that's in the process of being improved gets its own category. This includes things like improved (meaning it has access to roads and utilities) but undeveloped tracts of land, land in early development stages, subdivisions, and land being transformed for reuse (such as a former military base turning into a townhome community).

The most common way to invest in this type of property is through individual builder stocks or through funds that invest in an entire basket of construction-related stocks.

COMMERCIAL REAL ESTATE

Commercial real estate includes a wide variety of property types, such as:

- Shopping centers
- Hospitals and medical buildings
- Office parks
- Hotels and casinos
- Educational centers

Most investors (and some hold-all investments such as mutual funds and ETFs) categorize apartment buildings with more than five tenants as commercial real estate, even though they're technically residential real estate.

From a strictly investment perspective, commercial real estate has several benefits over residential real estate:

- More stable cash flow
- Longer leases (usually five to ten years)
- More opportunity for cash flow (more rental units than even a multi-family home)
- Economies of scale (lower per-unit costs, like buying in bulk)

Because it takes a lot of up-front cash to invest in commercial real estate directly, most beginners start investing here through REITs or crowdfunded real estate platforms.

INDUSTRIAL REAL ESTATE

Manufacturing plants, warehouses, distribution centers, and self-storage facilities fall under the category of industrial real estate. Though it's not the most interesting, this category is a rising star for real estate investors, largely due to the skyrocketing popularity of e-commerce. As more people shop online—and demand same- or next-day delivery—warehouses are cropping up all over the place to facilitate that service.

At the same time, manufacturing activity has been resurging, which also holds promise for investors looking to hold industrial real estate in their portfolio.

Cheaper to Operate

Compared to commercial real estate such as office buildings and hotels, industrial real estate usually costs much less to buy and maintain.

Examples of lower expenses (compared to other categories of investment property) include:

- Less cleanup and fix-up between tenants
- Cheaper vacancy costs (insurance, property taxes, heat)
- Less turnover

Those lower costs can translate into higher profits for investors.

Predictable Investment Income Stream

Industrial real estate comes with long-term lease commitments, and that means steady, stable cash flow for investors. Plus, these types of properties house the backbone of the economy: virtually everything we use has to be made, stored, and shipped.

In addition, it's easy to bring in different types of tenants (as long as zoning laws are followed) because industrial space lends itself to flexibility. For example, a warehouse could be rejiggered to be a warehouse with office space.

Best of all, this type of property offers the most income potential, due in part to its lower costs and locked-in leases. Industrial real estate also tends to have lower vacancy rates than other property types, so there's less time (if any) when it's not supplying income.

FIVE REASONS TO INVEST IN REAL ESTATE

Build Your Fortune

There are five key reasons to invest in real estate, and one potential disadvantage. That drawback is limited liquidity, which means you can't transform your investment into cash immediately (and sometimes not for an extremely long time). While that's true about direct real estate investing (buying a property to rent, hold, or flip), there are many ways to invest in real estate that eliminate that issue and still offer you all of the plusses of this resilient asset class.

IT'S REAL

Unlike the most popular investments—stocks, bonds, and mutual funds—real estate is tangible. You can see it, touch it, and stand on it. It's not an idea like bitcoin or stock options, and it doesn't exist only on a financial statement or an exchange: it's real. That means you have something of value even if the current market value falls to zero, unlike a stock or bond that would be worthless in a crash.

You can use your real estate even if the market considers it valueless. You can live there or turn it into productive space (using it to grow food, for example). And even indirect real estate investments are largely based on physical assets, which allow them to hold a more stable value even in a volatile market.

Limited Supply

There's a finite amount of usable land in the world, a limited supply. People need places to live and work, and as the population continues to grow, the demand for space grows right along with it. On top of that, we need land to produce food and deliver natural resources, from timber to oil to the elements that power our laptops.

Other investment assets are not finite. Corporations can issue more shares of stock. Governments and corporations can create more bonds to sell. And while land can be transformed to serve a new purpose, it can't be created from thin air.

More Control

When you own real property, you have more control over your investment than if you owned stock (a small portion of a company) or other paper-based assets. For example, you can do things to make your property more valuable, like spring for a new roof. You can affect the income by catering to more financially solid tenants and raising the rent. The flip side of that is your investment requires more active management. You have to maintain and repair it, or pay someone else to do so.

REAL ESTATE DIVERSIFIES YOUR PORTFOLIO

Diversification is a crucial part of successful wealth building. By combining many different types of investments in a portfolio, the risk of the total portfolio losing value is greatly minimized. That's especially true if your portfolio includes investments that don't act in the same ways as each other.

In theory, diversification helps smooth out the ups and downs of the markets and increase income potential. When one type of asset is drowning, another could be soaring, and that balance helps keep your overall portfolio steadier.

The Correlation Factor

Real estate doesn't act like other investments, and that holds true even if the real estate investment gets bought and sold like stock. That's because real estate has a low or negative correlation to many major types of investments. When you add real estate into a portfolio, it helps balance the ups and downs (called volatility in the investment world), which lowers your risk of total loss.

Here's how that works: say real estate has a low correlation to other assets in your portfolio. If those other asset values plummet, real estate will just dip slightly; if the other assets skyrocket, real estate will take a few steps up. It won't be as dramatic, and it won't be as heartbreaking.

Correlation

Correlation measures how two different investments move in comparison with each other. A perfect positive correlation means two investments rise and fall exactly alike, so if one tanks so does the other. A perfect negative correlation means that they move in opposite directions, so if one tanks, the other soars. Low correlation means they move the same way, but not at the same rate.

When real estate has a negative correlation with the rest of your portfolio, it moves in the opposite direction. If your other assets take a nosedive, your real estate investments will gain value.

Different Kinds of Real Estate Investments

Investing in real estate doesn't mean you have to own property, though that's what jumps into most people's minds when they think about it. There are several different ways to invest in real estate to help you build wealth, including owning any of the following:

- Residential rental properties
- Commercial properties
- Real estate industry–related stocks
- Mortgage-backed securities
- Mortgage debt funds
- Real estate investment trusts (REITs)
- Real estate mutual funds and exchange-traded funds (ETFs)

Inside each of those categories you'll find even more choices. For example, commercial real estate could be anything from a shopping mall to an office park to a hospital. Residential rental properties include single-family homes, apartment buildings, and retirement communities. So even within the real estate portion of your portfolio you can hold diverse investments.

Different Areas

In addition to diversifying among different types of real estate, you can also spread out risk by investing in several geographical areas. That way if one area gets hit hard by wildfires, storms, or a toxic chemical spill, you'll still have income-producing assets in other places that remain unaffected.

INFLATION CUSHION

Back in 1980, the median rent across the United States was $243 a month. Ten years later, that expense jumped to $447 per month. Fast-forward to 2015, and median monthly rent had risen to $942 per month. That's inflation: paying more money for the exact same thing. That's bad for tenants, but great for landlords and other real estate investors who can shield themselves from the inflation effect by passing it on to their tenants.

Inflation happens over time, with most prices tending to go up steadily. When that happens, your purchasing power decreases: $100 today buys more than it will twenty years from now. So for your money to really work for you, it has to earn at least as much as the inflation rate—but more is better.

The Inflation Rate

In the US, inflation typically runs at about 2 percent to 3 percent every year. Some years, though, inflation has been negative (that's called deflation). Other years, the rate has been much higher or lower than the norm: the inflation rate in 2015 averaged just 0.1 percent, while in 1990 it hit 6.0 percent.

Appreciation

In virtually all cases, real estate values appreciate (rise) over time. The longer you hold on to a piece of property, the more it will be worth. That makes real estate investing a natural foil for inflation.

Throughout the United States, residential real estate values have increased (on average) around 3.4 percent every year since 1991, and commercial property values typically increase 2 percent to 3 percent annually. Local markets, though, can see much bigger swings (in both directions). For example, according to ATTOM Data, home prices in the Seattle area are increasing more rapidly than in most of the US.

In addition, with real estate investments you have some control of your property value. You can make repairs, renovations, or additions that increase how much the property is worth.

Pass It Along

As mentioned earlier, investing in rental real estate can protect you from the effects of inflation: rising costs get passed through to tenants in the form of rent increases. This benefit works especially well when the property was bought with cash or with a fixed-rate loan. That means at least some of your costs will not increase even as you're able to charge more rent, helping further to protect your purchasing power.

This holds true with investments in commercial and industrial properties as well, something which surprises many novice real estate investors. Though these types of properties typically work with long-term leases, those agreements almost always come with "elevator" (also called "rent escalation") clauses, meaning the rent will increase over time. Sometimes that's at the landlord's discretion, and other times it's based on a formula. In either case, when property costs rise due to inflation, rents on these properties increase as well.

STEADY RETURNS, REDUCED RISK

Real estate investing offers multiple paths for earning income, some that deliver monthly and others that pay off over decades. Real estate assets are productive, bringing in regular cash (mostly from rents but possibly from other sources, such as timber sales, for example).

They also gain value over time, whether through market appreciation or more hands-on methods (such as renovation).

That's how investors can use real estate to balance their portfolios,
to stabilize returns with steady income, and to reduce their overall risk
by adding a safer asset class without sacrificing long-term growth. Most
stock investors are looking to capture rapid growth, a highly risky proposition. Bond investors are often looking for low-risk, reliable income, without the prospect for explosive growth. Real estate investors get the best of
both: stable current income and proven long-term growth potential.

The Volatility Factor

Real estate prices move around slowly, while stock prices move
around at rocket speed. That slow movement leads to less volatility in
real estate than the constant heart-wrenching ups and downs of the
stock market (think canoeing on a lake versus whitewater rafting).

That's why comparing returns on real estate investments and stocks
is like comparing apples to soufflés; they belong together under the same
general umbrella of assets, but they aren't alike in most other ways. To
make it a more useful comparison, experts look at risk-adjusted returns—
and that's where real estate investments outshine many other asset classes.

Risk-Adjusted Returns

When you invest money, you're taking a risk (that you'll lose your money) to
earn a return (more money). Riskier investments (such as stocks) usually promise higher returns to entice investors; after all, if the dollar returns were equal,
people would pick the safer bet. Risk-adjusted returns take that into account,
by looking at the real rate of return relative to its risk factor.

Stable Income Streams

Steady cash flows are a staple of most forms of real estate investing. Rental properties, whether you own them directly or through a fund, generate positive cash flow: rent payments cover property expenses with cash left over. That strategy works whether you have one rental property or invest in funds that hold thousands of them.

Even better, real estate investing offers *passive* income, meaning you just sit back and collect money rather than trading your time for money (as with a traditional job). That frees up your time for whatever you want to do with it, whether that's delving into other money-making ventures or traveling the world.

REAL ESTATE CREATES WEALTH

Building true wealth takes time—it doesn't happen overnight; in fact, in some cases, it takes generations. Many of America's wealthiest families have built their fortunes on a foundation of real estate. This sturdy asset class ranks among the top choices for members of the "three comma club" (billionaires) according to CNBC.

The Path to Wealth

Real estate is a proven wealth generator, providing all the ingredients needed to build a secure, income-generating nest egg. This single asset class offers investors a steady cash inflow (through rents), growth (through property value appreciation), and the opportunity to transform relatively small amounts of capital into much larger assets (through the use of leverage).

Consider this: if you have $20,000 to invest, you can either buy $20,000 of stocks or bonds, or put a $20,000 down payment on a

$100,000 property. Which seems like the most direct path toward wealth?

Holding On to Your Money

Real estate investing offers unmatched tax advantages that help you keep more of your earnings than you would with other types of investments. That brings the double benefit of increasing your net worth and leaving you with more cash to acquire more income-producing assets.

Examples of these unique tax benefits include (see Chapter 6 for full details):

- Depreciation (to reduce income taxes)
- Deferred capital gains opportunities through 1031 exchanges
- Tax-free cash flow through leverage
- No FICA taxes on rental income

These are just a few of the ways the tax code specifically benefits real estate investors, and these key advantages build up over time, giving you more capital to invest.

FOUR FACTORS AFFECT REAL ESTATE INVESTING

These Issues Influence Your Interests

Like every other type of investing, real estate investing is affected by a variety of factors. Some of these have a direct and obvious effect; for example, rising interest rates lead to lower property values. Others, such as changing demographics, have a less focused impact that affects values over time.

The Normal Cycle

The economy has a normal cycle, rising and falling in a predictable order (though not at predictable times). Every cycle has four phases: expansion, peak, contraction, and trough. If you know which stage the economy is in, you'll know what's coming next and be able to manage your investments appropriately.

These factors matter most when you're buying and selling real estate investments, less when you're holding on to existing investments. The main exceptions: trading-based investments like real estate–related stocks (such as construction companies) or real estate mutual funds and ETFs (exchange-traded funds), because they're also subject to stock market forces in addition to the factors that affect real estate.

THE ECONOMY

The overall state of the economy can have an enormous impact on real estate investing, but the type of effect depends on the type of investment. In general, real estate values will flourish in a robust economy and shrink in a sluggish economy. Real estate investments, though, can thrive in any kind of economy, and some do even better when the economy is down.

How a Slow Economy Affects Real Estate Investments

Different sectors within the real estate investment world aren't impacted the same way by changes in the economy. Some types of investment real estate are greatly affected during an economic slow-down; therefore REITs and funds specializing in these areas could see big price drops. Well-managed funds could snap up distressed commercial properties for a song, holding them in anticipation of the inevitable economic resurgence. Specific types of real estate that tend to buckle in a slow economy include:

- Hotels
- New home construction
- Shopping centers

Other types of real estate investments thrive in a down economy. For example, discount retailers see an uptick in sales as people adjust their budgets. Sin industries, which include casinos, also flourish as the economy worsens. Other recession-resistant property types are self-storage facilities and mobile home parks.

INTEREST RATES

Interest rates may be the biggest driver of the real estate market, because they directly impact the ability to buy property. That's especially true in the residential real estate market, important to landlords and house flippers: when rates are low, it costs less to take on a mortgage so people are more likely to buy, and that increased demand can drive up real estate prices. When rates begin to rise, mortgage costs go up, and that makes prospective homeowners less likely to buy, which can eventually lower real estate prices. That can be a double bonus for landlords, because any extra mortgage costs can be passed right through to tenants in the form of higher rent.

Rates also affect other types of real estate investments. REITs (real estate investment trusts), for example, offer a steady yield (sort of like interest on a bond). When interest rates drop, it makes those yields look better, so demand for REITs increases and their prices increase too. On the flip side, when interest rates rise, they can outpace that yield, making REITs look less attractive and lowering their market value. Those price fluctuations matter more if you're buying or selling—not if you're just sitting back and collecting the income from your REIT investments.

DEMOGRAPHICS

When it comes to real estate, people matter, and that's what demographics are all about. Essentially, demographics are statistics about the population and its subgroups that help describe group behaviors. Demographic factors include things like:

- Age
- Income level
- Marital status
- Occupation
- Family size

Real estate investors use demographic data to make decisions about things such as which types of properties to buy, which geographical areas to focus on, and how to make proactive investment choices based on upcoming population trends.

Big shifts in demographics can impact real estate trends for years, especially when it comes to residential rental properties. For example, as baby boomers move toward retirement, they could spark big changes in the real estate market. Baby boomers own about 40 percent of homes in the US; that could lead to a sell-off of larger family homes as they downsize to maintenance-friendly condo-style properties, increasing the number of single-family homes for sale. More homes on the market could lead to a sharp decline in home prices—bad for homeowners but a benefit for real estate investors looking to snap up residential properties.

Southbound

According to ATTOM Data, 62 percent of the growth in the real estate market will be heading south. Thanks to warmer weather, more affordable housing, and job availability, they predict more people will be moving to states like Texas, Georgia, and Arizona.

Other boomer-related trends could include shifts away from colder climates to more temperate areas, an increased demand for independent living communities, and a swing toward more convenient urban-style areas—all important factors for real estate investors to consider.

GOVERNMENT ACTIONS

Federal, state, and local governments can have a measurable impact on both demand for real estate and property values. They can boost demand in an area by offering tax deductions, tax credits, and subsidies to drive investor interest. They can steer policy and legislation for specific effect, like the introduction of the first-time homebuyer credit in 2009, which encouraged home sales in a sagging real estate market.

SALT Tax Deduction

The 2017 Tax Cuts and Jobs Act (TCJA) capped the total tax deduction for state and local taxes (SALT) to $10,000; that includes state and local income taxes and property taxes. The new cap could have a chilling effect on new homeownership, but it could also greatly benefit direct and indirect residential rental property owners. Plus, the SALT cap doesn't affect real estate investors, who can still deduct the full amount of taxes paid to support rental properties.

Opportunity Zones

The TCJA also created tax-advantaged Opportunity Zones to attract long-term investment in distressed areas and spur development and job creation. There are designated OZs in every state and five US territories. Investments must be made through Qualified Opportunity Funds (QOFs), which are basically holding companies set up to allow investment in eligible properties. Potential tax benefits include:

- Defer tax on *prior gains* until 2026.That means if someone sells stock and makes a $100,000 profit, then puts that money in a QOF, they don't have to pay taxes on the profit now.
- Exclude 10 percent of that prior gain *forever* if they hold the OZ property for at least five years, and 15 percent if they hold it for seven years.
- Investors who hold QOF investments for at least ten years won't have to pay any capital gains tax on profits when they sell.

As you might imagine, OZs have real estate investors across the US very excited—but the rules are brand-new, and no one has actually tested them out yet. Proceed with caution.

You can learn more about Opportunity Zones on the IRS website (www.irs.gov).

REAL ESTATE INVESTING IS IDEAL

Model Homes

Investing in real estate offers you a set of key advantages that you won't get with any other asset class. They're what make real estate investing IDEAL (an acronym that's been floating around for at least twenty-five years). IDEAL refers to the different ways real estate investing can help you accumulate profits and build wealth:

- **I**ncome
- **D**epreciation
- **E**quity
- **A**ppreciation
- **L**everage

Any one of these would make real estate holdings a valuable addition to any portfolio, and all five in one shot offers you accelerated wealth-building potential.

INCOME

Investing in real estate is one of the best ways to add a steady stream of income to your budget, whether you own physical properties or REIT (real estate investment trust) shares. Historically, real estate assets tend to generate constant, reliable income, largely due to rent payments.

For people looking toward retirement, this secure income stream can eventually replace salary; other commonly held retirement investments (such as stocks) don't hold the same promise. Building a portfolio of real estate investments can bring in cash flow from multiple sources, reducing your risk of falling short should any single investment run into problems.

How It Stacks Up

How does real estate–based *income* (not including growth or appreciation) compare to other types of investments? Consider this: as of December 2018, the dividend yield on the S&P 500 was 1.9 percent. The yield on a twenty-year Treasury bond was 3.01 percent. Yields on REITs easily topped 5 percent, with some ranging as high as 8 percent.

Rental Properties

If you own a couple of multi-family rental properties or office buildings, each individual unit sends income your way every month. Once you acquire enough properties and stable tenants, you'll build up a big enough income flow to replace the income from a regular job, so you can retire (no matter how old you are) whenever you want to.

On top of that, you're also amassing a huge source of untapped wealth. Should you need a large cash infusion for any reason (to pay for unexpected medical bills or to take an around-the-world vacation, for example), each rental property represents a virtual ATM: you can borrow against the equity or sell a property to get the cash you want.

REITs and Funds

REITs (real estate investment trusts) give investors the opportunity to take part in huge commercial, industrial, and residential real estate deals. Because of their special tax-advantaged structure,

REITs are required to pay out the lion's share of their profits as dividends to shareholders—a guaranteed income stream.

Real estate mutual funds and exchange-traded funds typically hold shares in REITs, and often pass at least a portion of those dividends along to shareholders. With funds, you'll typically have the choice of reinvesting those dividends to buy up more shares or receiving them as cash payouts.

DEPRECIATION

Depreciation is a special accounting expense that tracks the decline in asset value for things like wear and tear. For most assets, this makes sense: cars lose value as soon as they drive off the lot; machines in use for ten years start to break down. Most assets don't last forever. But for real estate, where the value of properties can just as easily increase, depreciation offers a rare beneficial disconnect: an expense on paper that transforms into real-life cash.

Not only does it reduce the taxable profits on your real estate investment asset, it may also offset a portion of your other income (this is a tricky tax area, so work with a qualified CPA to take full advantage). For example, if you had one property that ended up with a tax loss due to depreciation, and another property that produced taxable income, the loss from the first property could be used to decrease the profit from the second property. Plus, in specific cases (more on these in Chapter 6), you might actually be able to use that tax loss to reduce other types of income (like salary).

This tax jackpot works for indirect real estate investing (funds and REITs, for example) as well, though not in quite the same way for the investor. For example, because depreciation is not a cash expense, REITs appear to pay out more income than they earn, a boon to investors.

The Only Asset That Doesn't Depreciate

In the world of accounting, every asset depreciates except land. Therefore, with real estate investment properties, only the buildings on the land count toward depreciation expense. For accounting and tax purposes, the value of the land and the value of the buildings are kept separate. An experienced CPA can figure all of that out for you at tax time.

How It Works

Depreciation reduces income annually for tax and accounting purposes but unlike most other expenses it has nothing to do with actually spending money. This paper expense is based on the "useful life" of your investment property, which the IRS has determined as twenty-seven-and-a-half years. During that time, a portion (determined by IRS depreciation tables) of the property gets deducted from rental income, reducing the income tax bill. That translates into more available cash for the investor.

Here's a simplified example: say you had taxable rental profits of $100,000 this year, depreciation expenses of $10,000, and the applicable income tax rate was 20 percent. Without depreciation, you'd pay $20,000 in taxes (20 percent × $100,000). After deducting the depreciation expenses, the taxable income would be $90,000, and you'd owe $18,000 in taxes (20 percent × $90,000), a cash savings of $2,000.

Other types of real estate investments, including mutual funds and REITs, also get the benefit of depreciation expense. They pass that tax savings along to investors either through higher dividends or increased value.

The Recapture Trap

The depreciation advantage comes with a catch: when you sell the property, you have to "recapture" the depreciation expense you took. This can lead to a substantial tax bill in the year you sell. In addition to any regular capital gains taxes on the sale, you'd also have to pay your regular income tax rate (almost always higher) on the depreciation recapture. So if you had a gain on the sale of your investment property (your property sold for more than you paid), you'd pay tax on that at the lower capital gains rate. On top of that, you'd also pay tax at your regular income tax rate (which topped out at 37 percent in 2018) on the total depreciation deductions you'd taken over the years.

Luckily, there are ways to skirt that recapture, so you don't end up with a cash loss on the profitable sale of your investment property. (You'll find more information about all of this in Chapter 6.)

EQUITY

Equity refers to the portion of property that you own fully; it's the value of your property minus any outstanding mortgage debt. As you pay down the mortgage loan, your equity (your ownership percentage) increases. At the same time, property values tend to rise (at least over the long haul), which also adds to your equity.

As your equity increases, you can use it to build even more wealth. For example, you can borrow against existing equity to create a down payment for your next investment property. While that temporarily decreases your ownership stake in the original property, you still have the same total equity—but now you have two income-producing properties to show for it.

This also holds true for the underlying properties in indirect real estate investments like REITs. The holding company can use these methods strategically to maximize the value of its holdings and your investment.

Increase Value

There are two ways property values climb: one you can't control, the other you can. The housing market, both generally and in your property area, rises and falls and your property's value will probably ride right along with it. With the luxury of time, you can ride out the down trends until the market is ready for another upswing—and with real estate, it's only a matter of time before that happens.

The second way is to improve your property. Whether the changes you make are substantive, minor, or cosmetic, sprucing up the property will generally increase its market value, and possibly also its income-producing abilities. For example, you can add on more rentable space or make smart renovations that will allow you to increase the sales price and still attract plenty of buyers.

Decrease Debt

Debt is the other side of the equity coin, reducing your ownership stake. You can accelerate debt paydown by making extra principal payments. Not only will that immediately add to your equity, it will also reduce the interest portion of payments moving forward (interest is calculated based on the outstanding loan balance, so a lower balance means less interest). When a bigger portion of every payment is going toward principal, your equity will grow faster.

With rental properties, the income you receive from tenants will cover the mortgage—so those tenants are paying to increase your ownership stake.

APPRECIATION

Appreciation, where the value of an asset increases over time, is the opposite of depreciation. Real estate is one of the few physical assets that appreciates, which is one of the main factors making it a desirable investment.

There's only so much habitable land on the planet. Because land is a finite asset, demand will naturally outstrip supply; when demand outweighs supply, prices increase—it's basic economics.

That doesn't mean property values increase in a straight line; as we saw back in 2008, they can decline dramatically along with a troubled economy. Property values in different areas rise and fall in their own time. But overall, real estate values in the United States tend to appreciate, and that means tax-free growth for you (you don't pay taxes on appreciation until you sell, and never if you don't sell).

Property Trends

Supply and demand play a key role in real estate value: when end-user demand (more people want to buy houses) is higher than supply (houses for sale), market values rise, and the opposite holds true as well. Changes in an area can also drive demand, such as the arrival of new employers and shopping areas or changes in zoning laws. Real estate investors can track these trends using websites like Realtor.com (www.realtor.com), giving them a clearer picture of what's up-and-coming and which areas are cooling off.

Inflation

Inflation is a key factor that plays a role in real estate appreciation. Over time, inflation pushes up the cost of almost everything. That includes the materials needed to build, renovate, and repair homes or develop land, and real estate values as well. Over the long run, real estate values have at least kept up with inflation, often outpacing it (depending on the specific area).

LEVERAGE

One of the biggest advantages of real estate investing is the ability to use leverage: putting in only a little of your money and borrowing the rest to buy property. By coming up with a down payment and taking out a mortgage for the balance, you can invest in real estate for as little as 3.5 percent of the purchase price—a fraction of the cost. That means only a small amount of your money is tied up, but you still benefit as if you owned the whole property outright. You keep all of the income (like rent) the property generates. You claim all of the tax write-offs. You reap the rewards of soaring real estate prices.

You gain all those advantages with just a small investment, which leaves the rest of your money free to invest elsewhere. It's an important part of building significant wealth: using leverage to buy income-producing real estate assets.

Using Leverage to Create Cash Flow

Unlike other types of investments, direct investment in real estate (other than quick flips) gives you access to tax-free funds when you need to increase cash flow (money coming in) but not income. Here's how it works (and it works especially well with rental properties): you borrow money against the equity in your property, giving you access to the amount of cash you need. Because it's a rental property, the interest portion of loan payments is tax-deductible, lowering your overall tax bill. At the same time, rent paid by your tenants covers the loan payments over time.

This works especially well with:

- Properties that are completely or mostly paid off
- Rental properties that have stable tenants in long-term leases
- Fixed-rate loans

As long as the rental income (and your cash reserves) remains strong enough to cover the loan payments, you have access to tax-free cash flow when you need it.

CHAPTER 2

HOW TO PROFIT FROM RESIDENTIAL RENTAL PROPERTIES

Rental properties are one of the most stable ways to build wealth over time. By combining an asset with strong appreciation potential with a steady income stream, this investment offers both current financial security and long-term growth. Once you've got the knack, you'll be able to turn a single rental property into a real estate empire.

The idea of buying a property, getting it rental ready, and finding tenants can seem daunting. Taking it one step at a time can make the process flow more smoothly. Surrounding yourself with helpful professionals, familiarizing yourself with landlord legal issues, and carefully choosing the property and the renters will help ensure that your first dip into residential rental property is a profitable one.

PROTECT YOUR ASSETS

Work with a Safety Net

The first and most important rule of physical real estate investing—meaning you buy property—is to *never* purchase property in your own name. While there are a few different reasons for this, the most important involves personal asset protection, making sure that no lawsuits can touch anything you own personally (like your house, car, or bank accounts).

Other reasons for the "separate entity" rule (creating a holding company to own any investment property) may include:

- Special tax advantages
- Easier bookkeeping
- Simpler transfers to heirs

Next on the list for asset protection: insurance, and plenty of it. A lot can go wrong with residential rental properties, and proper insurance coverage is your first line of defense when expensive problems crop up.

The combination of a separate business and ample insurance offers the strongest protection against any of the many liabilities that could crop up, from tenant slip-and-falls to severe weather damage.

THE HOLDING COMPANY

One of the strongest tools in a real estate investor's kit is the holding company, a special legal structure that shields your personal assets (your house, car, bank accounts, etc.) from any problems having to do with your investment properties.

Two common types of business entities used for this purpose are limited liability companies (LLCs) and limited partnerships (LPs); in some cases, a combination of the two can offer an extra level of protection. Both entities offer maximum flexibility and pass-through taxation (the company doesn't pay income taxes itself; the income "passes through" to the owners' personal income tax returns). Which structure would work best for your situation depends on your circumstances, but both offer legal liability protection when set up properly.

In order for this strategy to work the way it's supposed to, you have to keep business and personal finances *completely separate*. That means, for example, you never make a rental property mortgage payment from your personal checking account, and you never deposit rent checks directly into your own bank account. If you need to move money around between the two, you have to do it officially—make a formal contribution to the company so it can pay the mortgage, or write yourself a check from the company after it deposits the rent checks. You also have to run the business professionally, keeping up-to-date records and following all the state regulations to lock in that liability protection.

LLC (Limited Liability Company)

LLCs are special business entities designed to protect the members' (the official name for LLC owners) personal assets from company-related lawsuits, and they've become very popular among real estate investors. You can form an LLC whether you're going it alone (a single-member LLC) or have partners. The company is formed according to state law and governed by a legal operating agreement, which is even more important for multi-member LLCs.

Any LLC member can take part in the day-to-day operations of the company unless the operating agreement specifically forbids it. That agreement also dictates how income is distributed.

Although there are state forms to fill out and fees to pay, LLCs require much less time, money, and paperwork than corporations but still offer their members solid personal liability protection.

LP (Limited Partnership)

Unlike an LLC, an LP requires at least two participants: one general partner and one limited partner, which can't be the same person (although a general partner can also be a limited partner if there's at least one other person involved). Only the general partners can be directly involved in running the business; limited partners are strictly forbidden from taking part in any of the day-to-day activities (which is why they're often called silent partners). Basically, limited partners put up the money, and general partners run the company.

General partners are 100 percent personally liable for any business obligations, which is why many LPs are set up with another company (often an LLC) as the general partner. Limited partners can't lose more than the money they contributed to the company, which can work well for a group of real estate investors who want to pool their money to buy properties without dealing with property management issues. The LP is formed according to state law and governed by a partnership agreement, which spells out specifics such as the general partner's responsibilities, ownership percentages, and how income will be distributed.

The Downsides of Holding Companies

Forming a holding company for your real estate investments offers solid legal protection, but it does come with some drawbacks.

First, it costs money to set up and maintain, and even more if you have an experienced real estate lawyer handle the paperwork. And to make sure your protection is as strong as possible, you want a legal expert on your side. This is one of the times that it's not better to DIY. In addition to having a lawyer set up your company (which can run anywhere from $300 to $2,000 depending on which state you're in and the lawyer you hire), there are ongoing state fees and taxes to contend with.

Second, you may need a CPA to handle the extra tax prep, depending on the type of holding company you form.

Third, it can be hard to get financing in the company name when you're just getting started. That means you may have to personally guarantee or co-sign for loans (which leaves you personally on the hook for mortgage payments). As soon as you form the company, apply for a credit card or line of credit in the company name and tax ID number. Even though you'll probably have to personally guarantee this credit initially, it will help the company begin to build its own credit rating for future loans.

DON'T SKIMP ON INSURANCE

A separate company protects your personal assets from being attacked, but it doesn't shield your rental properties from loss. The best way to do that is with the right insurance policies and enough coverage to make sure your company and your properties are protected against disaster.

The trick is to strike the right balance between the premiums you're paying and the benefits you're getting: too much coverage will shrink your profits and leave you cash poor, too little coverage could leave you financially devastated. You also want to make sure you have the right kinds of insurance for your investment.

Every property is different, and its unique features will determine the specific coverage you need. For example, a beachfront property calls for different insurance than a ski chalet. That said, there's some coverage that all landlords should have. Big picture: you'll need to make sure you have both property and liability coverage. Specifically, rental property investors should purchase these policies (some companies may combine them):

- Liability insurance (for both the property and the company)
- Fire and hazard insurance
- Sewer/septic backup insurance
- Personal property coverage (for any contents, such as furniture or appliances, owned by the landlord)
- Loss-of-income insurance (to cover lost rental income if the home becomes uninhabitable)
- Workers compensation insurance (if there are employees such as a building super or maintenance workers on-site)
- Umbrella insurance (to cover anything that slips through the cracks)

Some companies may lump these policies together in one big landlord policy, but make sure it includes all the coverage you want.

Depending on where the property is located, you may also want to consider flood insurance. Technically, that's only required if it's in a designated flood zone, but if the property is at the bottom of a hill or in an area that gets battered by heavy rains and hurricanes, consider adding this on. Floods caused by outside sources, rather than things like burst pipes or a leaking water heater, aren't covered by standard hazard policies.

If you aren't sure what kind of insurance your investment property needs, work with a professional who can walk you through the process. Visit the National Association of Insurance Commissioners at www.naic.org for advice and help finding a reputable agent.

PICKING PROPERTIES WITH STRONG PROFIT POTENTIAL

Reap Rewards with the Right Real Estate

Real estate investors are in it to make money. Reaching that goal starts with picking the right property, which can be tricky when you're new to the game. Before you buy, take the time to figure out what type of rental property you want, make a thorough rental budget, and scout out potential locations. You'll need to do your homework to select a property that meets your requirements and has all the features that most renters look for, like access to jobs and plenty of conveniences nearby.

WHICH TYPE OF PROPERTY?

Single-family homes are taking the residential rental industry by storm, but they're not the only (or necessarily the best) choice for a first-time landlord.

Multi-Family versus Single-Family

One of the first decisions you'll have to make is whether you want to invest in a single-family or multi-family property. Like the names state, single-family properties have one rental unit; multi-family properties have more than one unit. Both come with distinct benefits and drawbacks, and both make good choices for rental properties.

Benefits of single-family properties include:

- Usually easier to get financing
- Less maintenance
- No hassles between tenants
- Easier to sell

With a multi-family property, you can consolidate some of your expenses (because there's one roof and one yard, for example). They can be easier to manage than having several separate single-family properties, especially if the latter aren't near each other. It can be harder to get financing for a multi-family property, but a good down payment and a strong credit score may eliminate that issue. And if your main investment goal is maximizing cash flow, a multi-family property offers more opportunity for a stronger income stream.

House Hacking

Live in one of the units of a multi-family rental property, and your tenants will be paying your "rent." This setup also makes it easier and less expensive to get financing, which will increase your cash flow and your profits.

House versus Condo

For new real estate investors, condominiums can be a better way to wade in than single- or multi-family homes. Condos make good starter properties because you'll only have to deal with internal maintenance and repair issues, and the condo association will deal with everything else. That takes a lot off your plate, including:

- Trash pickup
- Landscaping
- Snow removal

On the condo con side, these smaller dwellings will bring in less rent and don't offer as much in the way of investment appreciation. They're also less likely to attract long-term tenants. Single people and new couples tend to rent condos. They're likely to change jobs and move more frequently, leading to shorter stays. Single-family homes will attract families, who tend to stay longer, especially when there are school-age children. Families tend to also be more financially stable, making them better tenants (especially when it comes to paying rent) than single people.

On the single-family home con side, they tend to cost more to buy, which means bigger down payments, loans, interest payments, and closing costs. They also require more upkeep than condos because you're responsible for the whole property, inside and out.

KNOW THE MARKET

Before starting any kind of business, smart entrepreneurs—and that includes rental real estate investors—take the time to do comprehensive market research. Even if you already have a particular neighborhood in mind, look at others to see if there's more profit potential somewhere else. Look at properties in and slightly out of your price range to get a full picture of the local market.

Rentability

You can pick the greatest property in the perfect neighborhood, but it won't matter if you can't rent it for enough to cover your costs and leave you with a tidy profit. Some common reasons a property will be tough to rent include:

- Lots of competition, which may force you to lower the rent
- Wrong kind of property for your target renter
- Needing to charge higher rent than the neighborhood normally bears
- A high (or growing) number of vacancies in the immediate area

You can increase your chances to get tenants in by offering incentives, like a free month's rent or utilities included.

Cash Sales Indicator

One clue to a good rental market: properties being snatched up for cash, which indicates investors. You can do a search at the local courthouse (part of the public record) to find out whether homes in the area have been selling for cash.

Rent Levels

The amount of rent you can charge will be determined by the area, and it has to be enough to cover all of your expenses and your desired profit to make the investment worthwhile. If the average local rent doesn't meet those criteria, you'll need to find a property somewhere else.

You'll also want to find out limits on rent increases, to make sure those can keep up with ever-rising expenses. If the neighborhood is up-and-coming, you can expect property taxes and other costs to increase quickly, and you'll need the rent to do the same.

KNOW THE NEIGHBORHOOD

To attract the type of tenants you want and have a near-zero vacancy rate, find a property in a high-quality, desirable neighborhood.

The neighborhood may also dictate the type of renters you attract. For example, if the property is in a college town, your potential tenant pool will be heavy on students, which means high turnover.

Schools Matter

If you're planning on renting to families, you'll want to make sure your property is in a highly ranked school district. The best property in an undesirable school district won't attract the tenants you're looking for, and it can also be harder to resell when you're ready to move on.

Check the Crime Stats

You wouldn't want to live in a high-crime area, and neither will most prospective tenants (no matter how low the rent is).

You'll want to specifically look into rates for vandalism (defacing property), petty crimes (like kids stealing things out of cars), and serious crimes (house break-ins, violent crimes), as well as whether those rates have been going up or down. Check in with the local precinct to find the inside scoop on neighborhood crime.

Expensive Areas

Some neighborhoods are more expensive than others and that means most things will cost more there. That's fine, as long as you can bring in enough rent to support the higher expenses you'll face. When you're deciding where to buy your rental property, look at all of your cost factors to make sure they don't outpace your rental income. While it's good to run a rental property at a loss for tax purposes, you want to make actual profits, bringing in enough cash to cover the property expenses and leave you with money left over.

Property Taxes

Property taxes can vary widely among neighborhoods and within neighborhoods. One thing you can count on: they're likely to increase every year.

According to WalletHub (https://wallethub.com) the average American pays $2,197 per year in property taxes—but that number is misleading. Effective real estate rates range from 0.27 percent in Hawaii to 2.40 percent in New Jersey (according to WalletHub). So in high-rate states, property taxes could severely eat into your rental property profits—another factor to consider when you're choosing an area.

UNDERSTANDING THE MORTGAGE PROCESS

The ABCs of Real Estate Loans

If you've ever taken out a home mortgage, you know how complicated it can be. In addition to compiling and filling out tons of paperwork, you also have to make key decisions about the loan itself. When you're taking out a mortgage for a rental property, the process is even more involved.

Your goal here is to borrow as little money as possible, which can substantially increase your rental profits and keep you from going under if you have a hard time finding a tenant. The less you borrow, the better loan terms you'll get, and the less interest you'll pay over the life of the loan, potentially saving you tens of thousands of dollars—and that savings can be used to invest in another income-providing property. To that end, you'll want to carefully research all of your loan options to find the best mortgage for your investment property. You can find reliable calculators online to help you compare rates and terms for different lenders.

WHAT YOU NEED FOR TRADITIONAL FINANCING

The cheapest way to finance your property is through traditional lending: a bank or credit union that does mortgage loans. But that savings comes with much higher requirements you'll have to meet, including a bigger down payment and a better credit score.

Before providing you with this kind of financing, the lender will want to know you're a good risk. That means you'll have to be prepared with a budget and a plan in place to cover potential problems (such as not being able to find a tenant right away). The lender will probably also want to see substantial cash reserves, so sock away as much money as you can before you start looking for loans.

A Big Down Payment

The amount of cash you'll need to bring to the table depends in part on your investment strategy—house hacking or straight landlord. Properties bought strictly for investment, non-owner occupied (NOO), call for down payments starting at 20 percent, and may be as high as 30 percent depending on the lender. Owner occupied (OO) properties face lower down payment requirements (in some cases as little as 3.5 percent of the purchase price), but that doesn't mean you shouldn't aim to put down at least 20 percent on your rental property. You'll also need enough cash to cover closing costs, which can come to 10 percent (or more) of the purchase price.

The OO versus NOO Difference

Say you find a multi-family property for $350,000. If you plan to live in one of the units, the down payment could be as small as $12,250. But if the property will be NOO, you could have to pony up as much as $105,000 for the down payment.

You Need Stellar Credit to Start

Before you start contacting lenders, check your credit report. To get the best deals, you need gold-star credit. Not only have lending standards gotten tighter (at least from the most reputable sources), investment-property loans are considered higher risk than live-in mortgages.

From your perspective, better credit means lower interest rates on the mortgages for your investment properties. That could translate into thousands of dollars of savings on every property, leaving you more room for profits.

HARD MONEY LOANS

If you're having trouble securing financing through traditional mortgage lenders, take a look at your hard money options. These deals are collateral-based, so they focus more on the property itself than on you, which can be especially beneficial for investors without perfect credit scores. In addition, because hard money lenders are so property focused, these deals can move much more quickly than the traditional thirty- to sixty-day closing timeframes common with traditional lenders. They're also more prepared to seize the property and sell it than a regular bank would be.

The Pros

This loan process is much simpler because you don't have to put together all of your tax and income information for a hard money lender. Typically, they'll look at your credit score but won't ask for any other documentation (such as proof of steady income). Instead, they'll focus virtually all of their attention on the property value and base your loan approval on that.

Plus, because hard lenders are usually individuals or small companies, they have more flexibility for working out deals than behemoth banks and mortgage lenders. For example, they may offer relaxed payment schedules or ramped-up payments depending on the particular situation, instead of being locked into cookie-cutter contracts.

The Cons

The biggest downside to hard money loans: higher interest rates, sometimes significantly higher. These loans also typically come with much shorter terms, often less than five years before the full balance of the loan comes due.

They also often call for bigger down payments for an LTV (loan-to-value) ratio. Whereas a traditional lender might be willing to finance 80 percent of a property, hard money lenders are more likely to finance only 50 percent to 70 percent.

WORKING WITH A PROPERTY MANAGER

Hand Off the Headaches

When asking rental real estate investors about their biggest newbie mistakes, the answer that comes back most often is, "I wish I'd gotten a property manager sooner." Hiring a property manager will make your landlord tasks a snap as long as you choose the right one. That takes some time, so start this process before the first tenants move in.

WHAT THE PROPERTY MANAGER DOES

Property managers handle all the heavy lifting and day-to-day tasks of being a landlord so you don't have to. Specific responsibilities will vary depending on the type of property you own but they tend to fall into the same categories:

- Dealing with tenants
- Handling the property finances
- Maintaining the property

Managing Tenants

Your rental property can't turn into a gold mine without tenants. A good property manager will find, screen, and select the best tenants for your property. They'll take over handling background and credit checks and verifying references. With experience on their side, many property managers have an instinct for selecting long-term, reliable tenants who don't cause problems. Once they've chosen tenants, the property manager will handle the lease signing and security deposit.

After tenants move in, the property manager will hear and deal with complaints, maintenance requests, and emergencies (such as burst pipes). They'll handle problems between tenants (in multi-family dwellings).

When the lease is up and not renewed, the manager will deal with all of the move out issues, from damage assessment to deposit return. In the case of a tenant who refuses to vacate, the manager will know exactly how to handle an eviction.

Setting and Collecting Rent

Experienced property managers know the score when it comes to setting rent. They know the area, the property type, your budget, and the prospective tenant pools. With that information, they can come up with appropriate rent that won't scare away tenants and still leave you with profits—a skill that could take you years to develop. They can also adjust the rent up or down as the situation calls for; they know the rules about rent increases (which may be strictly controlled by state or local law), and they can adapt rent to changing economic circumstances to make sure your property stays occupied.

Once you have tenants in, the property manager deals with collecting rent, and that includes making sure tenants pay in full and on time. They set dates, grace periods, and late fees—and strictly enforce those rules so you don't get stuck in a cash flow situation.

Property Maintenance

Once you hire a good property manager, it's their responsibility to make sure the building is safe and regularly maintained. Whether they have in-house taskers or hire out, they'll make sure everything necessary gets done in a timely and cost-effective fashion. This includes things like:

- Landscaping
- Snow removal
- Trash pickup
- Pest control
- Repairs

Even with an OOP

You can use a property manager even if you live in one of the units (an owner-occupied property). In fact, that can make your living situation easier because other tenants will call the manager—and not you—when things go wrong.

FINDING POTENTIAL PROPERTY MANAGERS

Once you've decided to hire a property manager, it's crucial to find the right one. This person (or company) will be a long-term partner and will have an enormous impact on your investment success (and peace of mind). Take your time with this decision: do research, conduct interviews, and do a little snooping. After all, you'll probably be partnered up with your property manager for a long time, so you want someone who clicks with you personally and professionally.

Read the Agreement

Once you sign a property management contract, you're locked in for the term of the agreement. Because this will impact every aspect of your investment success (from happy tenants to solid profits), make sure you read and understand everything in the contract. If anything seems unclear, talk to your attorney before signing.

Check These Sources

First stop: your real estate agent. They can offer you a list of property managers they and their clients have worked with successfully. From there, talk to other landlords you know in the area, and ask who they use to handle their properties. Make sure to ask what they like (and don't like) about this manager, and what kinds of problems they've had. If you get the same take on a management company from several different sources, chances are it's true.

You can also search online for property management companies in your area, but be wary of online reviews. Check the Better Business Bureau for any company that sparks your interest to see if any complaints have been filed against them.

Like any other professional, property managers have specialties, and you'll want to find one who specializes in the type of rental property you own; someone who runs apartment complexes isn't the best choice for your single-family home.

Check Their Work

One of the best ways to see how a property manager works is to see how they're handling other properties. For example, look at the "for rent" ads they're placing for your competitors to see if they look professional. Look at a couple of properties they manage to see if they look well kept.

Even more important, talk with tenants. You're hiring the property manager to make your life easier, and that includes keeping your tenants happy. Steer clear of any property managers where:

- Complaints and repairs aren't addressed promptly.
- The manager is hard to reach.
- Tenants aren't renewing their leases because of the management.

Eleven Questions to Ask

During your interview with any prospective property manager, make sure to cover all of these key questions:

1. How long have you been managing properties?
2. What types of properties do you manage?
3. What licenses and certifications do you hold?
4. Do you have a thorough understanding of landlord-tenant law, including fair housing practices, eviction procedures, and safety codes?
5. How long does it typically take you to fill a vacancy?
6. How do you vet prospective tenants?
7. How many tenants have you evicted in the past six months?
8. What services do you provide?
9. What are your fees and how are they charged?

10. Where are the property funds held and how are they handled?
11. How often do you perform property inspections and do preventive maintenance?

These are the minimum questions you need to have answered before selecting a property manager. You can find a more thorough list on the BiggerPockets website (www.biggerpockets.com).

Check Certifications

Many states require property managers to hold some type of license of certification (usually to be allowed to show rental properties). Check that any prospective property managers hold the specific documentation required by law (you can do this on the state licensing website).

Find out whether they belong to a reputable trade organization that requires training, certification, and continuing education. Applicable organizations include the National Association of Residential Property Managers (www.narpm.org) and the Institute of Real Estate Management (www.irem.org).

WORK WITH A TEAM TO MAXIMIZE SUCCESS

The Building Bunch

Investing in residential rental real estate is a team sport, so don't go it alone. Assemble a group of professionals who can fill in any knowledge, skill, or experience gaps. That will help ensure that you don't get in over your head and get stuck with problems you don't know how to solve—it's always more expensive to call someone in after there's a problem than to get a pro to help you avoid problems in the first place.

Start developing relationships with key professionals before you buy your first property. They can help you navigate the investment from start to finish and handle everything that comes up in between. Long-term relationships with real estate agents, lenders, and other experts will serve you in several ways, from increasing your profitability to connecting you with the resources you need to remain successful.

Real Estate Agent

A real estate agent who works with investors (and not just homeowners) can be the centerpiece of your team. In addition to helping you with property selection (the foundation for your success), the real estate agent can also help you find suitable tenants. They'll also have contacts with lenders, lawyers, and management companies—anyone you might need to help make your investment successful.

Real estate agents know neighborhoods. They know what prospective tenants are looking for, which areas have the fiercest competition, and what properties are ripe for profits.

Lender

Once you've decided to invest in rental real estate, you'll want to start developing relationships with potential lenders. The process works differently than when you're getting a regular home loan, so you don't turn to your home mortgage broker unless he also has substantial experience working with real estate investors.

For your investment properties, you'll want to connect with a lender who regularly works with investors and will help you grow your real estate portfolio...as well as offering you the lowest possible interest rates. If you have no existing connections, you can start your search online using a rate comparison tool (like the one at Bankrate, www.bankrate.com). Be aware that many lenders limit the number of investment loans, so you'll want to ask how many loans you could carry if you plan on expanding your real estate empire.

ROUND OUT YOUR TEAM WITH THESE PROFESSIONALS

In addition to your A-team and property manager, you'll want to connect with other professionals to provide key skills. Make sure anyone you hire has experience working with residential rental properties; you want experts who really know what they're doing to make up for any gaps not covered by you or the rest of your team.

At the very least, you'll want to find a lawyer, an accountant, and a handyman (yes, even if you're using a property manager) on whom you can depend when you need them.

Lawyer

Landlord and tenant laws can be complicated, and having a competent rental real estate attorney on your side can help you avoid potentially costly lawsuits. Your attorney can also help:

- Set up your holding company correctly
- Draft leases
- Deal with property closings and title issues
- Navigate federal, state, and local laws
- Review and revise the property management contract

CPA

Find a CPA with rental property experience (even better, one who owns residential rental property); not all accountants know the ins and outs of this business, and the difference could end up costing you thousands in taxes. Most people go to the accountant at the end, when it's time to deal with taxes—that's a mistake. Connecting with the accountant *before* you buy a property can vastly improve the project profitability and help you avoid costly mistakes that could eliminate potential tax breaks.

Your CPA can help you:

- Create a property budget
- Deal with estimated tax payments
- Set up and manage retirement accounts

- Analyze complicated financing options
- Handle all the tax returns

Handyman

Things go wrong with properties all the time. If you don't have the time or background to deal with repairs, find a competent general handyman to work with. He'll handle a wide variety of issues, from hanging fixtures to winterizing to basic repairs. Some handymen can also take care of basic plumbing and electrical issues, but don't use them instead of licensed professionals for big jobs. It can be hard to find a reliable and reasonably priced handyman, so start your search early.

TENANTS AND LEASES

Landlord Rules

To be a successful landlord, you need reliable tenants who always pay their rent in full and on time. That calls for careful and thorough screening, and a painstakingly clear rental agreement—the lease—that spells out exactly what you and your tenants expect from each other.

Before you start screening tenants, come up with a list of questions that you'll ask *everyone*, and make sure none of your questions are illegal (for example, "Where do your kids go to school?" is an illegal question). Next, you'll move to the formal rental application, and follow up by verifying everything on there. You'll choose your best candidate—and hope they choose your property. From there, it's time to sign the carefully crafted lease and let your tenant move in.

KNOW THE LAW

As a landlord, you must be careful to treat every prospective tenant equally; it's the law. The rules are laid out in the federal Fair Housing Act, which was created to help ensure that landlords don't discriminate against people simply based on specific factors, including:

- Race or color
- Religion
- Sex
- National origin
- Disability
- Familial status

You can find all the details of the Act by visiting the US Department of Housing and Urban Development (HUD) website at www.hud.gov.

Follow State Law Too

In addition to the federal law, many states (and some smaller localities) have their own fair housing rules that landlords must follow. Before you create a lease agreement or begin interviewing potential tenants, make sure you're fully aware of the state and local rules and regulations for rental properties.

A Word About Eviction Laws

Though you hope it will never happen, there may come a time when you're forced to evict a tenant. Each state has its own specific rules and procedures that landlords must follow in order to terminate a rental agreement. Those rules differ based on the reason for eviction: either nonpayment of rent or violating something in the lease (for example, having a dog in a no-pets-allowed apartment or subletting without permission).

The rules about eviction for late or unpaid rent vary pretty widely but cover four basic topics:

1. When you can send a "pay rent or quit" notice (*quit* means "move out" here)
2. How you have to serve the notice (usually either in person or by mail)
3. How long the tenant has to come up with the rent or be evicted
4. Your options if it's not the first time this has happened

Most states give the tenant a window of time (usually somewhere between three and thirty days) to try and fix or stop their lease violation or move out before the landlord officially evicts them. Some states let landlords terminate the agreement right away without giving the tenant a chance to fix the problem.

TAKE TIME CHOOSING TENANTS

Good tenants can make your landlord experience smooth and profitable; bad tenants can destroy property, skip out on rent, and make you wish you'd invested in the stock market instead. The key to zeroing in on the best tenants is research.

You want to look for tenants with a proven track record of both financial responsibility and personal responsibility. People who've changed jobs frequently or moved around a lot probably won't make good tenants; when you're looking for stability, past commitment history tells you what you can expect going forward.

To gather the basic information you need, create a comprehensive rental application for each tenant to complete (if more than one person will be named on the lease, have each fill out a separate application). Then take the time to follow up and verify that information before you settle on a tenant. And always trust your gut: even when a tenant looks great on paper, if your instinct says something feels off, move on.

The Rental Application

A thorough rental application can act as a great tenant-screening tool. It helps you organize and evaluate the information you collect on prospective tenants and provides the data and permission you need to run credit and background checks. To cover the costs of those checks, most states allow you to charge application fees, though some limit how much you can charge.

A basic rental application asks for information such as:

- Name and Social Security number
- Complete contact details
- Employment history (company name, salary, dates of employment, full reference information)
- Rental history (at least three years, including landlord contact information and reason for leaving)
- Basic screening questions (such as, "Have you ever declared bankruptcy?" or "Do you smoke?")
- Signature that explicitly (a) verifies the information on the application is true and (b) gives permission for credit, background, and reference checks

Keep every rental application, even for the people who don't become your tenants. Then if a rejected applicant tries to sue you (usually under the Fair Housing Act), you'll have a solid paper trail of protection that spells out why someone else was a better candidate.

To streamline this process (and make things much easier for you), consider using an online rental application tool. These can help you stay organized, allow applicants to upload documents (like W-2s for income verification), and save on paper storage space. Websites such as Zillow (www.zillow.com) offer free screening and rental application services for landlords.

Verify Everything

Once a prospective tenant fills out a rental application, it's your job to verify that information. Call the employer to confirm the prospective tenant's job status, earnings, and how long she or he has worked there. Contact prior landlords (ideally, at least two) to see what kind of tenant he or she was. If the tenant is including alimony or child support in her income, ask to see the court order and six months of bank statements showing that money was received regularly. (In many states you can't discriminate based on source of income—but you don't have to rent to someone who can't prove he or she is actually receiving that income.)

No matter how much you like a prospective tenant, do your homework. Verifying the information will save you a lot of hassle (and potentially eviction proceedings) down the line.

Run a Credit Check

Before you rent to anyone, you need to know that he or she can and will pay the rent. The best way to find that out is by running a credit check. You can either do that on your own (which is inexpensive or sometimes free) or hire a service (which costs more but usually includes a thorough background check as well).

To DIY the tenant credit check, contact at least one of the three major credit bureaus (Experian, TransUnion, and Equifax) and request a credit report. Experian (www.experian.com) offers free tenant screening credit reports to landlords. TransUnion (www.mysmartmove.com) offers tenant screening services starting at $25 each. Equifax (www.equifax.com) tenant screening reports start at $15.95.

Before you can order credit reports, you need explicit permission from every tenant who's at least eighteen—and you should check this for all adult tenants. To pull the report, you'll need basic information from the tenant's application, including his or her full name, birthdate, and Social Security number. Also, all adults who will be living there should be named on the lease, even if they're not technically responsible for the rent; i.e., occupants rather than tenants.

Do a Criminal Background Check

Criminal history is a matter of public record, for even minor offenses. You'll want to look into this thoroughly for the safety of your property, your other tenants, your maintenance workers, and yourself. A complete background check calls for looking at several sources, including:

- Criminal court records searches at the local, state, and federal level
- An "offender search" through the Department of Corrections
- The sexual offender database

Some of those searches are free; others may cost between $10 and $30 (on average). Since there's not a nationwide criminal database, running a thorough check can be tricky—especially because criminals may lie on their rental applications.

Consider Going with a Pro

It's tough, time-consuming, and potentially expensive to do a thorough background check, especially if the prospective tenant has lived in several different states. Make your life easier by using a full screening service like SmartMove (www.mysmartmove.com) or MyRental (www.myrental.com).

LEARN LEASING LINGO

Once you've selected the perfect tenant, it's time to bring out the lease (here, the word *lease* also includes rental agreements). This is a binding legal document that sets out the rules that you and your tenants agree to follow, and it should include plenty of details, from the monthly rent amount to exactly how long the tenant can live in the property. You can make the lease as long or short as you like, but make sure that it includes at least the following information:

- The full names and signatures of all adult tenants
- The time period of the tenancy
- Rules of occupancy (who's allowed to live there, which protects you against subletters and permanent guests)
- The rent amount, including when it's due and how it should be paid
- Fees and deposits
- Landlord entry, including advance notice rules
- Repairs and maintenance, including which responsibilities fall to the tenant
- Restrictions on illegal activity
- Pet policy
- Any additional restrictions, like no smoking or rules about home businesses
- Rules about common areas, like parking lots or swimming pools

Make sure your lease completely complies with state and federal law. If you don't want to deal with the hassle of drafting your own lease, you can find templates online at websites like Nolo (www.nolo.com) and LegalZoom (www.legalzoom.com).

Lease versus Rental Agreement

What's the difference between a lease and a rental agreement? Time. Rental agreements typically go month-to-month, renewing automatically until you or your tenant terminates it. Leases usually come with a term of at least one year.

Security Deposits

You'll collect and hold a security deposit to make sure the rent gets paid and to help ensure the tenant (or their kids, friends, or pets) doesn't damage the property—or to cover the damages they cause. Every state has different rules for how much you can charge, where that money has to be kept, how you can use the money, and when you have to return the deposit (or what's left of it after reasonable deductions). Those rules vary pretty widely: Arizona, for example, caps security deposits at one-and-a-half times rent and gives the landlord only fourteen days to return the deposit after the lease is up; Maryland allows for security deposits of twice the rent, and requires that the deposit be returned in forty-five days. Some states require landlords to hold security deposits in interest-bearing accounts and that interest goes to the tenant. These rules are very strict, so make sure you check the state law where the property is to avoid potential legal hassles.

Should You Allow Pets?

Many new landlords jump to a "no pet" policy. Before you decide, consider all the pros (yes, there are pros!) and cons of allowing pets.

Here are some ways you could benefit from a pet-friendly rental property:

- **Charge higher rent.** If the area is flooded with no-pets-allowed properties, you might be able to charge higher rent (sometimes *hundreds* of dollars more) by allowing pets.
- **Bigger tenant pool.** According to the American Pet Products Association, 68 percent of US households have pets. A study by Firepaw.org found that only about half of all landlords allow pets. The math is clear: allowing pets gives you access to more tenants.
- **High-quality tenants.** Several surveys show that pet owners tend to make more money than people with no pets. Pet owners typically stay in a rental longer because it can be difficult to find another pet-friendly property. Both of those are big plusses for landlords.
- **Avoids sneak-ins.** Allowing pets lowers the chance that people will sneak in unapproved pets (and they do). Having it all up front lets you know what pets will be on the property, and lets you charge a pet deposit or monthly pet fees (depending on state law) to protect you from any animal damage.

That's the biggest downside, animal damage, but it's not the only con to consider:

- **Damage.** Scratched-up floors, chewed-up molding, pee stains—all of these are common issues with pets, and they can be very costly to repair.
- **Noise.** Animals make noise, sometimes very loud noise (like incessant barking). They also run around, sometimes in the middle of the night, which can disturb other tenants. That could lead to lost tenants if those pets are too disruptive.
- **Liability.** If you allow pets—especially dogs—there's the risk that they'll bite someone, including you, another tenant, or a

maintenance worker. Make sure your insurance covers this potential liability and whether the policy contains limitations (like where the bite occurs) or exclusions (like a "dangerous breeds" list).

DON'T UNDERESTIMATE RENTAL EXPENSES

Counting Costs

The vast number of expenses associated with rental properties can shock new landlords. Many jump in thinking that as long as the rent covers the mortgage payment and property taxes, they'll be reeling in profits. That can lead to huge financial issues, even bankruptcy, because they aren't prepared for all the costs they're going to face. Taking the time to make a complete rental budget that accounts for regular and extraordinary expenses will help you make sure you don't get caught short, and that your property will earn profits.

On top of that, your rental properties count as a business for tax purposes. No matter how they've been set up, at the end of the year you'll need to report their income (or loss) on a tax return.

Include All Rental Income

Seems like a no-brainer: the money your tenants pay every month counts as rental income. That's true, but it's not the only thing that could count toward income. For example, if you have an arrangement with your tenant that he or she does yard work in exchange for a rent reduction, the value of that yard work counts as part of your rental income (even though there's no actual money involved).

DEDUCT EVERY EXPENSE YOU CAN

Most new landlords don't realize the wealth of expenses linked to rental properties; they assume the expenses are limited to what they can deduct on their own homes. But one of the biggest benefits of owning rental properties is the combination of real-world cash profits and on-paper tax losses. That means you could end up with positive cash flow every month without having to pay taxes on it.

At every stage of the game, you'll have certain guaranteed expenses, including mortgage interest (if you borrowed money), property taxes, insurance, and property maintenance. Most other expenses will change based on whether or not the property is rented.

Getting the Rental Ready

To attract high-value tenants and get a lease signed as quickly as possible, your property needs to make a good first impression. That means boosting its "curb appeal," which can include things like planting flowers, trimming trees, painting rooms, and refinishing floors. It also means making sure all plumbing, wiring, and appliances are in perfect working order, and possibly even updating older equipment before it gives out.

In addition to the sprucing-up costs, you'll also be able to deduct things like insurance, utilities, taxes, and other ongoing expenses even before your property is ready to be rented. Finally, this category also includes the fees for any permits, licenses, or certifications required before the property can be rented.

Before It's Rented

Just because you have a tenant-ready apartment doesn't mean it will be rented as soon as you list it; some properties sit on the market for weeks or months before a tenant moves in. All the money you spend to get a tenant into the property goes into your expense list. That can include things like the cost of:

- Paid listings (in newspapers or online)
- Hiring a property manager
- Researching the local rental market
- Advertising (such as signs or flyers)
- Real estate agents

As long as your property is available for rent, all of those expenses will flow into your financial statements and your tax return.

Once You Have a Tenant

After a tenant has signed a lease and moved in, you'll have new (or higher) expenses to deal with:

- Repairs
- Wi-Fi (if included with the rent)
- Water bills
- Utility bills (if included with the rent)
- Maintenance (new light bulbs, HVAC filters, etc.)
- Trash and recycling removal

That's for tenants who don't cause any issues. Expenses may be higher with problem tenants who consistently clog toilets, leave food out (attracting bugs or rats), or actively cause damage.

A CLOSER LOOK AT DEPRECIATION

Real estate investors have access to a special expense that reduces income on paper without actually costing any money. Depreciation is an accounting expense based on the idea that any kind of physical property (*except land*) loses value to wear and tear over time. It has nothing to do with changing market values, lousy tenants, or superior handymen; depreciation is all about time.

Here's the basic idea: instead of taking the entire property as an expense all at once (the same way you'd count an electric bill as an expense), you divide it up over time. That way, you take a portion of the property as an expense every year over its "useful life."

Rules to Depreciate

As you'd expect, the IRS has pretty strict rules surrounding depreciation deductions, and you have to meet all of them to qualify. In order to legally deduct depreciation:

- You own the property (loans are okay).
- The property is being used to make money (even if it's not making money now).
- The property has a "measurable" life (which all buildings do).

As long as you meet all three requirements, you can reap the enormous tax benefits of depreciation expense.

The Math

To calculate depreciation, you need to know your *basis* in the property. Basis means the total cost to acquire the rental property, which typically includes the full purchase price (even if you borrowed some of it) and most closing costs. From that, you have to subtract the value of the land (because land does not depreciate for IRS purposes) to get the basis for the building. If you make any permanent improvements to the property (putting on a new roof, for example, is considered permanent; repainting rooms is not), those get added on to the basis.

The IRS timeframe for depreciating residential rental property is twenty-seven-and-a-half years, but it doesn't happen evenly over time; it starts high and gets lower every year. The agency provides depreciation tables that help you figure out what portion of your property can be expensed every year.

Even though your accountant will be taking care of this, it's still important to understand how depreciation works so you'll know why it looks like your investment is losing money even though you have positive cash flow.

CHAPTER 3

BUILD WEALTH FLIPPING HOUSES

House flipping skyrocketed after 2008, when millions of homes went into foreclosure and investors scooped them up for pennies on the dollar. Then, within a few years, came the resurgence of the TV shows (there are dozens of them now) where a house was bought, fixed, and flipped in under an hour—or so it seemed. Those shows sparked flip excitement, and suddenly everyone who'd done some puttering around the house was looking for property to flip in the hopes of scoring huge profits. Most of them lost money and got out. Some people stuck around, learned a lot, and slowly became successful real estate investors. With lessons learned, you can start investing in flip houses the right—and profitable—way from the start.

THE ART OF FLIPPING

As Seen on TV

It looks super easy on TV: buy a house, slap on some new paint, and sell it right away for a huge profit. They make it look fun and stress-free, but that's TV; the real-life version is very different.

TWO WAYS TO FLIP

There are two basic types of house flipping:

1. Fix-and-flip: You buy a low-priced fixer-upper, make some key improvements, and sell it for a profit.
2. Live-in and flip: You buy an underpriced property in good structural shape, spruce it up over time while you live there, and sell when the property value has increased.

Most investors go for the straight fix-and-flip—it's what all the shows are about—and this chapter will focus mainly on this strategy. This is not an arena to enter casually (especially with gargantuan dogs like Zillow joining in), but it is possible to collect big profits with the right approach.

If you're not in a rush, and the property you choose doesn't have any issues that make it uninhabitable, the live-in and flip strategy may work better for you. Both strategies come with profit *and* loss potential, but you can tilt the odds in your favor by doing your homework before you buy.

The Hold and Flip

There's a third way to invest in flip properties, but it's less popular because you have significantly less control over the outcome. With a hold and flip investment, you buy an underpriced property in an *expected* up-and-coming neighborhood and hold it until property values increase. Without the time to wait or the means to write it off if the increase never materializes, this would not be a good investment strategy.

Why Fix-and-Flip?

If you're handy around the house and love DIY home projects, a fix-and-flip investment could be perfect for you. These projects need to move quickly to be profitable and require a major time commitment (even when you don't plan to do most of the work yourself). If you love a challenge, have good credit and a pile of cash, and know your way around tools, this could be an ideal investment opportunity for you.

Expect your first flip to be a learning experience rather than a profit bonanza (practically no one makes a lot of money on their initial flip). Pick up as many skills and make as many connections as you can to make your second flip a winning investment.

Why Live-In and Flip?

With this strategy, you buy a house to flip, and live in it while doing the repairs. This can be a great way to get your feet wet in the house-flipping space because it gives you more time to get things done. Plus, when you plan to live in the house, it transforms a lot of the finances normally associated with house flipping. For example, you can get a regular home mortgage and use regular homeowners insurance, both of which can be much less expensive than if you were doing a standard fix-and-flip.

Plus, if you live in a home for at least two years, then capital gains from the sale may be completely excluded from taxation. That means taxes won't eat a huge chunk of your profits, leaving you with more cash to buy your next hold-fix-flip.

BUY LOW, SELL HIGH

The idea behind profiting from house flipping is the same as with other types of investments: sell it for more than you paid, and pocket the difference as profit. According to ATTOM Data, the average house-flipping *gross* profit (before any expenses were taken into account) for the second quarter of 2018 across the US was $65,520. That sounds like a lot, but it's down about $4,000 from earlier in the year, and the numbers vary widely depending on where you are. Keep in mind that a lot of people lose money or break even when they flip a house, and (again) that's before taking their expenses into account.

There are a lot of factors that play into this, but the most important is choosing the right property, followed closely by having an accurate flip budget.

The 70 Percent Rule

To limit the financial downside while maximizing your profit potential when you flip a house, you need to know your costs before you buy a property. To start, you need to know how much the property is really worth so you don't end up overpaying. Then, you need a realistic estimate of the repairs and renovations the property needs to be attractive for buyers. Armed with that information, you can calculate the perfect price for your flip property by using the 70 percent rule.

The 70 percent rule is a guideline to help real estate investors make the best deals. According to this rule, the purchase price shouldn't be more than 70 percent of the after-repair value (ARV, how much the house should sell for after all the repairs are made) minus the total cost of those repairs.

The Need for Speed

One key to maximizing profits involves what happens in between the purchase and the sale and how long that takes. In house flipping, speed is your friend on the *selling* side. The longer you hold the property, the smaller your profits will be. That's because you'll still be paying all the costs associated with holding the property, which could include:

- Mortgage interest
- Property taxes
- Homeowners association fees
- Utilities
- Insurance

The sooner you sell, the sooner you shed all of the costs that are eating into your profits. And the longer the house is on the market, the more likely you'll have to drop the asking price, which deals another blow to your profits.

FOUR RULES FOR A SUCCESSFUL FIX-AND-FLIP

Do This for a Fun Flip

House flips are more likely to fail (be unprofitable) than succeed, especially for beginners. Renovations always take longer to complete and cost more than expected, which can leave investors in the hole if they haven't anticipated setbacks. In addition, it's much harder to fix-and-flip a house than it looks on TV, and many novice flippers are shocked when they find out the extent of necessary work and the possibility that they could lose money on the deal.

To give yourself the best possible chance of success, you'll have to take a hard look at your goals, abilities, and availability. Learn everything you can before you snap up what seems like an ideal property and end up stuck with a loser.

KNOW YOUR COMMITMENT LEVEL

Before you dive in to the fix-and-flip life, sit down and think about how much you're really willing and able to commit to this undertaking. If you're going all in on a DIY rehab, make sure you have the skills and experience you need to be successful. Renovating a house involves grueling physical work and dedication to the project. So honestly answer these questions before you decide to take this path:

- Are you able to do contractor-quality work?
- Do you know which permits you need?

- Are you aware of all local building codes?
- Do you have subcontractors to handle repairs you aren't qualified to make?
- Do you have enough cash saved to cover higher-than-expected costs?

Even if you're not planning to do all the work yourself, fixing and flipping a house requires a huge time commitment, and the more involved you are in the process, the bigger that commitment will need to be. While it is possible to work a full-time job and rehab properties, it's not an ideal situation. Properties undergoing renovations need daily check-ins, preferably when the contractor is on-site. If you can only get to the property after work and after the contractor (or foreman) has left for the day, you're more likely to run into problems and delays—and that will lead to shrinking profits.

Consider a Flip Mentor

Seek out a successful flipper, and ask if she or he'd be open to mentoring you. You'll gain valuable knowledge and experience that would otherwise take years (and lots of failure) to learn. To increase your chance of "yes," consider offering the flipper a small portion of the profits on your first successful flip.

Gather Pros to Cover the Gaps

Chances are, you're not a real estate agent and a CPA and a real estate lawyer and a contractor. For any area in which you're not an expert, hire a professional. There are a lot of intricacies involved in a successful house-flipping investment, and if you don't know what you're doing, your dreams of plentiful profits can turn into mountains of debt.

If you are planning on doing as much of the fix-up work as possible on your own, don't cut costs when it comes to make-or-break parts of the project. Even seasoned contractors call on licensed professionals to fill in experience gaps. Make sure you know what kind of help you'll need, and take steps to secure it before you get started.

Have a Cash Stash

Financing your flip with cash (or mostly cash) vastly increases your profit potential. Not only will you save thousands of dollars in loan fees and interest, you'll also be in a better position if the house takes longer than expected to fix or flip (which almost always happens, especially in the beginning).

Remember, to be profitable, the sales price has to exceed the total purchase price, carrying costs (insurance, loan interest, utilities, etc.), and renovation expenses. Cutting down borrowing costs—interest, loan application and settlement fees, mortgage insurance—leaves more money to invest in renovations. Plus, having a sizable down payment for the property can get you better terms for any money you do need to borrow.

MAKE THE RIGHT RENOVATIONS

It's tempting to create a dream house with hardwood floors and top-of-the-line appliances, but that kind of thinking will put you on the fast track to flip failure. When it comes to renovations, you want to make only those that will add value—not just look good. Small tweaks can make a big, cost-effective impact: for example, painting and putting new hardware on cabinets can add as much value as installing new cabinets but at a fraction of the cost.

Remember, the less you spend on renovations, the bigger your investment returns will be. Before you dive in, learn how much typical projects cost. Know what you'll spend to re-carpet a house, update old wiring, and spruce up landscaping.

While every flip project is different, some upgrades that almost always add value include:

- Updating kitchen appliances
- Upgrading the washer and dryer
- Repainting inside and outside
- Adding closet space
- Building a deck
- Adding a bathtub (if there isn't one)

Depending on the area, bringing in some green energy features can increase the home value—but make sure there's a positive "going green" vibe in the neighborhood before you take on the extra expense.

Repairs Are Not Renovations

While you may decide to go lower budget on renovations, don't skimp on necessary repairs. Anything that involves building codes or safety should be done professionally, and anything that's actually broken should be fixed.

First Impressions Matter

The first thing someone sees when they're viewing your property is the outside ("curb appeal"). A neat yard and a fresh coat of paint make a good first impression, and convince the buyer to walk inside.

Simple touches can help add to the curb appeal, and most of these can be done (as needed) without shelling out a lot of cash:

- Make sure the trim work is freshly painted
- Paint the front door or add new hardware
- Install outdoor lighting
- Plant seasonal flowers
- Repair cracks in the driveway and walkways
- Put in a new mailbox

These minor fix-ups won't bust your budget, but they will help draw buyers to the house.

PRICE THE HOUSE PROPERLY

It can be tempting to price your flip house based on how much money you want to make, but if you don't want the house to sit there unsold you'll need to come up with a realistic, competitive price. For example, if you pick up a property in a neighborhood where most houses are selling for $150,000 to $175,000, you won't be able to sell it for $200,000. In fact, you probably will end up selling somewhere toward the lower end of that range.

To avoid excessive lag times and the drag of having to keep lowering your price (which can make potential buyers think there's something wrong with the property and bypass it completely), set your price in keeping with the appropriate comps in the neighborhood. You can also order an appraisal to get an objective view on the property value.

Be aware that other things will come into play when you're ready to sell. For example, homes sell better in spring than winter. A glut of homes for sale in the same area makes it harder to get your asking price; a lack of for-sale homes will make it easier. Bottom line: be realistic about the probable sales price range *before* you buy your investment property.

Strategic Pricing

When people are looking for houses, they usually search in a price range. Those ranges are often measured in ten- (sometimes five-) thousand-dollar increments (such as $220,000 to $230,000), so a home price at the top of a range gets as much play as a lower price. If you decide to lower your price, move it down enough to change its range (for example, lower it to $219,000 rather than $220,000); that way your audience will be expanded to include people searching in the new range.

Pay Attention to Comps

Before you set a price, look at what other homes in the neighborhood are selling for, especially those that have similar characteristics to your investment property. The best way to do that is by viewing "comps," data from a comparative market analysis (CMA), easily available to real estate agents. To make your own accurate comp list, include these filters in your search (on any real estate sales website):

- Within a half-mile radius from your property
- Current listings (no older than three months)
- Similar square footage (within 10 percent)
- Similar age

You can also go online and get a "Zestimate" based on Zillow's (www.zillow.com) individual home market value estimator. (While you're there, make sure that all the information listed is correct, since millions of people use Zillow as a starting point for home buying.)

Consider Incentives

In an area with similar homes for sale, offering an incentive can set your property apart from the pack. Possible incentives include offering six months of prepaid homeowners association dues, paying buyer closing costs, or paying for the home inspection.

Get Help from Your Real Estate Agent

Real estate professionals are better at pricing houses than you are. They know how to move properties fast—but are motivated to get the highest price reasonably possible because their commission is based on it.

Your real estate agent is familiar with the market and can come up with a competitive price that still lets you reap some profits. He or she will also know exactly how to stage the house for maximum buyer appeal.

In addition, your real estate agent has access to the CMA and knows how to use it to your advantage. They can also weed through the comps for currently listed properties, pending sales, and properties that have already sold (or been taken off the market) to come up with a beneficial price point.

PROTECT YOUR INVESTMENT

For your protection, it's best to not purchase property in your own name, but use a holding company instead. That serves the dual purpose of shielding your personal assets from any liabilities arising from the business property (like a contractor being hurt) and protecting your investment from being lost to a personal judgment (like a tax lien).

At the same time, you can reap other benefits by creating a holding company for your investment properties, such as:

- Extra tax advantages
- Simplified accounting
- Streamlined transfers to heirs

The key to cementing that protection is to keep personal and business finances completely separate all the time. That means, for example, never using a personal credit card to buy renovation supplies at Home Depot. If your flipping business needs cash, make a formal contribution to the company rather than paying the contractor with your personal check.

In addition, treat your business like a business: run it professionally and in accordance with all federal, state, and local laws. Keep your bookkeeping up to date. And while you can form these companies DIY, it's better (especially if you're working with partners) to have an experienced real estate lawyer set it up for you.

Make Sure to Be Fully Insured

A lot can go wrong during renovations, and bulletproof insurance coverage will be your first line of defense if disaster strikes.

Insurance for fix-and-flip properties can be expensive, making many flipping newbies shy away from complete coverage. The goal is to balance the cost of premiums with the benefits you're getting: buy the right kinds and the right amount of coverage.

This can be tricky, because some insurance companies won't want to cover vacant properties, and coverage you do find can be much more expensive than regular homeowners insurance. In addition to vacant (or unoccupied) property coverage, house flippers should consider purchasing:

- Fire and hazard coverage
- Sewer/septic backup coverage
- Vandalism and theft insurance
- Errors and omissions (E/O) coverage (a professional liability insurance)
- Workers compensation insurance (if there are employees like a building super or maintenance workers on-site)
- Flood insurance (depending on where your property is situated—like at the bottom of a hill or in a flood plain)
- Umbrella insurance (to cover anything not covered by other policies)

Some companies may combine these policies in one big policy, but make sure your coverage is as comprehensive as you need.

You can look online to check out real estate investment insurance offerings on the National Real Estate Insurance Group website (https://nreig.com). If you aren't sure which insurance coverage your investment property needs, work with a professional who has experience with flipping. Visit the National Association of Insurance Commissioners at www.naic.org to find a reputable agent.

BUILD A FLIP TEAM

Assemble the Crew

The most successful flippers surround themselves with a team of qualified professionals. While that may seem like unnecessary spending, it can save you a great deal of money—and time—over the long haul. Professionals can help you build a solid liability shield, develop a realistic flip budget, secure financing, control costs, keep repairs and renovations on schedule, and help the eventual sale close without any drama.

Having the right people on your side will help you navigate any pitfalls that crop up (and something always goes wrong), and help you build the confidence and experience it takes to make you profit from your investment. Key members of your flip team could include:

- A real estate agent
- A construction contractor
- A lawyer
- A CPA (certified public accountant)

With a seasoned team to guide you, even your first flip will go more smoothly. Make sure that you're comfortable with each team member, and that you verify that they have experience with rehabbing and flipping properties. It can take time to build these relationships, so be patient, because the time you put into building your team will be worth it if you decide to continue flipping properties.

REAL ESTATE AGENT

A successful house flip starts with buying the right property, and a real estate agent with access to real estate owned (REO, foreclosed properties that did not sell at auction) inventory lists will provide invaluable assistance in your search. There are real estate agents who specialize in distressed or bank-owned properties, and adding one to your team could give you the inside track on potential gold mines.

In addition, real estate agents often act as the hub for real estate investors, connecting them with lenders, contractors, lawyers, home inspectors, and other professionals.

Working with an REO Real Estate Agent

Some real estate agents specialize in REO properties and work directly with banks to help them get rid of inventory. You can easily find these agents by doing a simple online search for your target location. Often, their websites will include blogs, which can give you real insights into their experience and style. Make sure the agent has actual REO experience (rather than just using it as a keyword) because the process is different than a regular home sale.

On the bank side, you'll face a sales committee and a team of lawyers who may push to change terms once a deal is already in progress. The bank will also be less open to compromise than a regular home seller. Having an experienced real estate agent on your side can make negotiations with the bank go much more smoothly, and even encourage the decision makers to accept your offer.

Six Ways a Real Estate Agent Can Help You Flip

The number one reason to work with a real estate agent is that she can help you find and snap up properties with the most potential.

Develop a good relationship with the agents who work the neighborhoods you're looking into, and your real estate investment career will be off to a good start. Experienced agents offer a wealth of benefits, including:

1. Inside track on distressed properties.
2. In-depth knowledge of neighborhoods and school zones.
3. Staging the property (inside and out) to spark maximum interest: it's hard for buyers to picture themselves living in an empty house. Staging is a way of furnishing and decorating in an appealing way that helps them visualize living there. Effective staging can get a house sold more quickly.
4. Properly pricing the property for a quick, profitable sale: experienced agents have an instinct for pricing, high enough that you make money (and they do too) but not so high as to turn off potential buyers. They know which comps matter and which features add value.
5. Listing the property *everywhere*: in addition to the websites you'd have access to, real estate agents can put your house up on the MLS (multiple listing service) for maximum coverage. They'll know which disclosures (if any) you're required to make.
6. Connections with contractors and lenders.

Most successful flippers team up with real estate agents early on, and continue to develop relationships with agents to get early access to the best deals.

CONTRACTOR

Hiring a reliable, experienced, *licensed and insured* contractor can make your project profitable; hiring the wrong contractor can leave you broke.

Arrange face-to-face meetings with each contractor you're considering, and treat those meetings like job interviews. Make sure that you're comfortable with the contractor and feel good about adding them to your team. Keep an eye out for these red flags:

- The contractor shows up late for the appointment.
- He's rude to you or dismissive of your questions.
- He refuses to provide a written estimate.
- He doesn't ask you any questions.
- He doesn't return calls within a reasonable timeframe.
- He tells you the job doesn't require any permits (most renovations and major repairs do).

Trust your impression. You're hoping to embark on a long-term relationship with this contractor, so if he makes you uncomfortable at the outset, move on to someone else.

Ask These Questions

During your meeting with the contractor, make sure to ask at least these key questions:

- How long have you been doing this?
- How many projects like mine have you worked on?
- Which permits will the project need?
- Will you set up the inspections and obtain the permits?

- What insurance coverage do you have?
- Will you be bringing in subcontractors?
- How long do you estimate this project will take?
- What's the best way to contact you?
- Where will materials, supplies, and equipment be stored?
- How do you deal with changes? (For example, if the tile you chose isn't available.)
- How often will you be on-site?

In addition, you'll want to ask for at least three references from customers who are in no way related (personally or through a business affiliation) to the contractor.

Why the License and Insurance Matter

Any contractor you work with—and any subcontractors he hires—should be appropriately licensed according to state law. If they're not, you could suffer financial consequences.

You may not be able to get favorable loan terms or proper insurance coverage for your property without proof that you're working with a licensed, insured contractor. In addition, you could face fines (depending on state and local codes) if you allow an unlicensed contractor to work on your property.

Before you hire someone, verify the contractor's license with the state board. You'll also want to check that he's licensed to perform the specific work you need (for example, a licensed electrician shouldn't be hired to do plumbing work).

Any contractor you hire should show you proof of his general contractor liability insurance. That insurance should cover any personal bodily injury and property damage that occurs during the project. It's also important for the contractor to have personal liability and workers' compensation insurance (for his crew). Ask to see his certificate of insurance before you sign a contract.

Get Written Bids

Reputable contractors will provide detailed bids in writing (if a contractor won't, pass). You'll want to see specifics, including:

- Project start date
- How many days (or hours) she'll work on your project each week
- Full price estimate
- A detailed (color, size, model, etc.) list of materials that will be used
- How she wants to be paid
- Expected completion date
- Whether the job includes cleanup (hauling trash, cleaning spills or stains, etc.)

It can be tricky to compare bids to one another, especially if the contracts don't list the same line items in the same way. One way to get around that: create a spreadsheet (your accountant can help with this) for the bids, so you can see a more direct comparison.

Lowest Doesn't Mean Best

It can be tempting to go with the lowest bid—after all, the less money you spend, the more money you'll make—but sometimes a low bid is a red flag. If a bid comes in much lower than expected, ask the contractor to explain why. If his answer doesn't make sense, move on.

Because time is an important factor in house-flipping profitability, insist on including a penalty for work that's not completed on time (for example, $50 deducted from the contract price for each day over the deadline).

Be Clear About Payments

For your protection, do not pay your contractor with cash (and beware of any contractor who insists on that). For small repairs and renovations, the contractor should accept checks or credit cards. For larger renovations (as is the case with most fix-and-flips), you'll probably need to arrange for financing.

In addition to agreeing on a project price, you'll need to work out a payment schedule with your contractor and put that in writing. Tie payments to specific completion goals or defined blocks of work (for example, a payment of $5,000 when the master bedroom work is completed). That helps protect you from a calendar-based schedule where you may be paying for work that has not been done yet. Make sure to also include information about what will happen if particular materials are unavailable, which will change the project cost (called a "change order").

Most states allow contractors to ask for upfront payments to cover material costs, but those down payments are strictly limited. The website www.usa.gov/state-consumer lists all State Consumer Protection Offices, which makes it easier to find the right information source. In addition, most states don't allow for final bills to be substantially larger than estimates unless you've approved the increases.

LAWYER

An attorney who specializes in real estate investments and asset protection can be a valuable addition to your team, especially if you're working with partners or private lenders. When you're flipping a house, you need the strongest possible protections in place because uninhabited properties can be legal landmines. Lawyers familiar with this industry will know the best ways to protect you from all the what-ifs (kids sneak into the house and get hurt, a contractor falls off a ladder, etc.) and make sure contracts are fair and legal before you sign them or turn over any money.

Here are just a few of the things a qualified attorney can help you with:

- Set up your holding company (or companies)
- Settle any title issues
- Review and revise contractor and lender contracts
- Let you know what permits and licenses are required
- Advise you on multi-state legal requirements

Make sure any attorney you hire in this capacity has a long and strong background in asset protection and real estate law.

An Ironclad Liability Shield

Before you buy your first house to flip, have your lawyer set up your holding company, a legal entity that will hold your properties to protect your personal assets from any liability issues that arise. Without that barrier, anyone who gets hurt on your investment property (whether or not they're supposed to be there) could sue you personally. A properly created holding company can protect you from financial ruin by keeping your personal assets separate from your investment assets.

Your attorney will help you figure out the best structure for your holding company based on your unique situation. In some cases, multiple holding companies or a combination of legal structures may be required to protect each investment property (when you have more than one at a time) from liabilities arising out of the others.

Clear Title Is Crucial

In the world of distressed properties—where many house flippers reside—title issues can get complicated. Sellers may not always have clear title to the property (due to liens or inheritance issues, for example), and that can lead to a lot of problems for you unless you have a competent attorney to sort everything out.

Common issues that can come between you and a good title include:

- Tax liens
- Creditor liens
- Heir groups (where one wants to sell but others don't)
- Easements
- Deed restrictions (like not being allowed to obstruct a neighbor's view)
- Property restrictions (which may limit changes to the property, like adding a shed)
- Property allowances (for example, there's a lake on the property and the previous owners granted access to the whole neighborhood)

Your attorney will either straighten out the impediments to clear title or advise you to walk away from the property. He can also handle the title insurance to protect you against issues that arise after the sale has been finalized (for example, one creditor lien was overlooked during the title search).

What Is the Title?

In real estate, title refers to legal ownership and use of a specific piece of property. Any time a property is sold, a title search is conducted to make sure the person selling the property is the true legal owner.

CPA

A good CPA can mean the difference between paying a boatload of taxes and preserving more of your precious cash. That's just the beginning of the ways her financial expertise can help you become a more successful flipper.

As your house-flipping empire grows, your CPA can:

- Help determine the most lucrative business structure
- Help you put together a business plan
- Create a realistic flip budget
- Monitor project costs
- Work with lenders to help you secure funding
- Keep track of project profitability
- Handle payroll and independent contractor payments
- Determine estimated tax payment requirements
- Help you set up and fund retirement savings

The key is to find an accountant experienced in working with real estate investors.

Not All CPAs Know Real Estate

Real estate investors are eligible for several targeted tax breaks, but your CPA has to know what she's doing to help you take full advantage of them.

A Plan and a Budget

Your accountant will help you create a focused business plan and a realistic project budget to maximize profits. It's especially important to get help with these if you haven't ever created a business plan or budget before; these tools are vital to your real estate investing success and need to be done before you buy your first property.

Creating a business plan forces you to look at every facet of your real estate investment and can help you uncover potential pitfalls before you get started as well as help you secure financing. The plan will help you focus your goals and expectations, solidify timelines, and identify areas where you'll need outside expertise.

The budget (which will flow into your business plan) will help you figure out how much property you can afford, sort out necessary and unnecessary repairs, and anticipate realistic renovation costs. A thorough flip budget includes:

- Investment property purchase price and settlement costs
- Loan costs (such as application fees, points, and lifetime interest)
- Repair and renovation costs (based on estimates from experienced contractors)
- Inspection fees
- Staging costs

- Selling costs (including real estate agent commission and other closing costs)
- Professional fees
- Insurance
- Property and school taxes
- Utilities
- Income tax provisions

Unexpected costs can tank your investment returns, and an experienced accountant can help make sure you include all potential expenses in your flip budget.

Don't Forget Taxes

If you decide to DIY your flip budget to save on professional fees, don't forget to include taxes. This category encompasses federal, state, and local income taxes that you may have to pay if your flip is profitable. Even if you do the budget on your own, talk to your CPA about minimizing the tax bite before you buy your first property.

SNIFFING OUT BARGAINS

The Bargain Basement

You're in the flip business to make money, and that starts with buying bargain properties—not cheap properties but undervalued ones (and there's a *huge* difference). New real estate investors can get drawn in by an ultra-low home price (sometimes buying sight unseen), excited by the idea of a quick fix-up and an instant sale for far more than the purchase price. But if a house is priced well below market and has not sold, there's a reason—and it won't be one that a new flipper would want to take on.

Your path to success starts with a house that's worth more than its price and will gain even more value when you make strategic renovations. That path ends if you buy a cheap house that turns into a ravenous money pit, where you'll be lucky if you end up breaking even. Be careful in your bargain hunting to find the best deals—even if they're not the rock-bottom cheapest.

BUYER BEWARE

Homes can come with some nasty hidden surprises, from toxic mold to about-to-burst pipes to cracks in the foundation. Any of those (or surprises like them) could bring your real estate investing career to a sudden halt, as they can decimate your financial situation. For these reasons, and the dozens of other issues that could crop up, it's crucial to get a home inspection for any property you intend to purchase.

These profit-smashing issues are even more likely to crop up with distressed properties (like foreclosures or tax sales) where the people who lost their house have no incentive to leave it in good shape. In addition, if a house has been sitting vacant, problems may have gone unnoticed, giving them time to worsen.

Avoid These Red Flags

No matter how much you like a house or think it could bring in big money, avoid buying potential flip properties that have even one of these red flags:

- Mold
- Old or damaged wiring
- Lead paint
- Roof issues
- Structural issues (such as a cracked foundation)
- Termite damage

Any of these issues requires a huge investment of time and money, two things you don't have to spare when your goal is to flip the house.

When Inspection Isn't an Option

Sometimes it's just not possible to get an inspection before you close on a house, and that's more likely to be true with distressed properties bought at auction. In fact, in some cases you won't even be able to see inside the house before you buy it. This increases the risk that you'll end up losing money on the deal, since you won't know what's wrong with the house and won't be able to budget accurately for renovations and repairs. Without knowing the real *value* of the property, it's difficult to know whether you're paying a reasonable amount for the house.

New home flippers should avoid buying any properties without an inspection. After you've had a few successful flips and built a solid flip team, you might be willing to take the gamble.

FORECLOSURES

A house goes into foreclosure when the owner can't make his or her mortgage loan payments. The house gets repossessed by the lender and put up for sale at an auction in order to satisfy the outstanding loan. Most often, these homes have been abandoned, sometimes by very angry former homeowners. Other times, people refuse to leave the homes, meaning you may have to deal with eviction issues (which can add to your costs).

In many cases, you'll have to make offers on the house without seeing inside, so you won't have any idea what condition the house is in; they've often been neglected, damaged, or ransacked and require a lot of fixing up. Sometimes the sale will go through without the buyer having been allowed to get the home inspected. Plus, the house may also be subject to additional liens; it's not uncommon for someone who stops making mortgage payments to also stop making property tax payments, for example. Finally, many foreclosures are sold for cash only, so you may need to bring a lot of money to the table.

Potential Loan Issues

If you're planning to finance a foreclosure property, you may face some additional hurdles. For one thing, the property may not pass the lender's inspection guidelines, making it ineligible for financing. Plus, because prices can be bid up at auction, your purchase price may exceed the home's appraisal value, which can severely limit your loan amount. Finally, foreclosed homes may come with title issues, which hold up closing; since house flipping is a speed game, this can drastically alter your timeline and profit potential.

The Move to REO

Foreclosure homes go first to auction, and any that aren't sold there end up in the bank's inventory as real estate owned (REO) properties. These homes come with the same cautions as standard foreclosures plus more: they've been vacant longer, meaning they'll probably need a higher level of cleaning, repairs, and renovations, which can add significant costs to the flip budget. Banks may require large (often non-refundable) deposits when you sign a purchase contract (sometimes as high as 5 percent of the total purchase price), so you'll need plenty of cash on hand to go this route. That deposit may have to be paid before you're allowed to inspect the property, so if you walk away from the deal, you'll lose the deposit (which may be the wisest move if the property's a wreck). On the plus side, a home that's gone REO usually comes with a clear title (which is not always the case with foreclosure properties).

While not all REO properties end up selling at ultra-low prices, they're more likely to be sold below market value because:

1. They're vacant, which can lead to problems (vandalism, etc.).
2. The bank has to keep up with property tax, insurance, and utility payments.
3. The bank has to keep the property maintained so it doesn't deteriorate.

Banks do not want to be in the homeownership business, so they're motivated to sell...but they're also motivated to squeeze every possible penny out of buyers.

Finding Foreclosed Homes

The best way to find quality, undervalued homes in foreclosure is through an experienced real estate agent. They're often familiar with bank (pre- and post-) auction inventory and will be able to find a property that matches your requirements.

If you're going DIY to find foreclosed homes, you can look online; there are several legit sites that list homes in foreclosure and REO status. The downside: you only have pictures to go by, and pictures can lie about the true condition of the property. Check out these sites to start your search:

- RealtyTrac (www.realtytrac.com)
- Redfin (www.redfin.com)
- Trulia (www.trulia.com)
- Fannie Mae HomePath (www.homepath.com)
- US Department of Housing and Urban Development (www.hud.gov)

All of these sites have extensive lists of foreclosed homes in virtually every price range, so you'll have a lot of properties to choose from.

TAX SALES

Tax-sale homes are similar to foreclosed homes in that the home was repossessed from an owner who stopped making payments; in this case, property tax payments. There are two types of tax sales—tax lien sales and tax deed sales—and they work differently. With a tax lien sale, you basically take over for the taxing authority and now have the right to collect the tax payments plus interest. In a tax deed sale, you're buying the property and its unpaid tax bill.

Both sound simple, but they're not quite as straightforward as they sound. Either can make a good investment in the right circumstances, but they can also be quite cumbersome to deal with if things go wrong.

Tax Lien Sales

Most states allow tax lien sales, but the rules are slightly different everywhere. Generally, here's how a tax lien sale works:

- A homeowner skips property tax payments, triggering a state "waiting period" that can last up to a few years.
- The lien gets auctioned off and goes to the highest bidder.
- The homeowner has to pay the new lien holder the back taxes plus interest; if he or she doesn't, the lien holder can foreclose.

It's actually better from an investment standpoint to collect the taxes plus interest rather than go through the expense of a foreclosure, especially when the property is likely to be in bad shape.

Tax Deed Sales

Tax deed sales are also usually auctions. Here, though, the property has typically been seized by the government and sold for (at least) the total amount of back taxes, interest, and fees. In most cases, though, the sales price gets driven up by bidders, sometimes substantially, despite the fact that they usually cannot see the inside of the house before they bid.

If you win a tax deed auction, you immediately own the property. That means you've just bought a distressed property sight unseen, without a home inspection. It could be chock full of code violations, damage, or hazards (like radon gas or black mold). So while the purchase price may seem like a steal, you could be paying much more than the property is actually worth. Take this path with extreme caution.

LOCATION MATTERS MORE

"Where" Trumps Everything

The first rule of real estate—Location! Location! Location!—holds especially true for house flippers. It's normally the most important factor for determining the property value, so you need to be intimately familiar with the neighborhood before you buy into it.

The location holds the context for your flip: Is it in an area that attracts seniors or young families? Do the neighbors commute to the city or work in town? Knowing the type of people attracted to the location will help you target buyers more effectively, and dictate which features you'll highlight when you're ready to sell.

SEARCH FOR POSITIVE FEATURES

When it comes to buying houses, most people want the same things: safety, convenience, and good neighbors. When you're scoping out locations for a potential flip property, focus on areas with these desirable features:

- Easy access to highways and public transportation
- Good schools
- Nearby shopping and restaurants
- Low crime rates

Think about what would attract your desired buyers to a neighborhood, and make sure the area you're interested in fits the bill.

Safety Check

You can find information about neighborhood crime rates by visiting CrimeReports (www.crimereports.com), SpotCrime (https://spotcrime.com), and the US Department of Justice's National Sex Offender Public Website (www.nsopw.gov).

Convenient Access

Think about the services you use regularly—your potential buyers will probably need them too. They'll want the same kinds of stores and services nearby; no one wants to have to drive an hour to get a pizza. Make sure that at least some of these standard conveniences fall within a reasonable distance from the potential flip house:

- Gas station
- Grocery store
- Post office
- Bank
- Hospital
- Pediatrician
- Daycare providers
- Dry cleaner
- Gym

Other positives (but not necessarily must-haves) include good local restaurants, nearby parks (especially with playgrounds) and bike trails, and libraries.

SCHOOLS RULE

Considering that 62 percent of homebuyers have children under the age of 18 living with them (according to the 2018 *Home Buyer and Seller Generational Trends Report* put out by the National Association of Realtors), the local school district can make or break your flip house's salability. A more highly ranked and desirable school zone can add thousands to your sales price and attract more potential buyers.

Even buyers who don't have children will consider school districts; after all, they're likely to sell at some point too.

Schools Impact Property Values

Not only do homes in good school districts tend to draw higher sales prices, they also tend to hold value better than homes in less desirable districts. That holds true even in periods of declining home prices. When you're looking into potential flip properties, check the local school ratings—especially for elementary schools (which have the biggest effect on home values). You can find comprehensive ranking information on the web at GreatSchools (www.greatschools.org) or SchoolDigger (www.schooldigger.com).

Keep the Comps in the District

To get the most accurate idea of comparable sales, make sure to look at homes in the same school district. Neighboring homes that fall into different districts won't offer you a true comparison. Similar houses less than a mile apart can have substantially different selling prices all because of school boundary lines. In fact, according to research by Pro Teck Valuation Services, a preferred school zone can bump up a home's market value by as much as 58 percent.

LOOK FOR A SPARK

When you're buying a house to flip, look for a neighborhood that people are going to want to move into—find a neighborhood where positive change is in process or expected. A spark of impending growth can help you get a good deal on a house in an up-and-coming neighborhood before it catches on. The trick is to spot the sparks before other investors (and a good real estate agent is a major asset in this arena).

Growth Indicators

There aren't always neon signs to indicate a neighborhood will soon undergo a growth spurt. However, there are some key factors that can help you identify an up-and-coming neighborhood ripe for investment.

- Consistently increasing rents
- Transit systems added or revamped
- A trend toward younger demographics
- Major retailers moving nearby

Some real estate investors go for the "Starbucks factor." Companies like Starbucks study market data extensively—so if they're moving into an area, chances are it's a smart place to buy a flip property.

Avoid a Negative Catalyst

Certain events can trigger a mass exodus from an area, resulting in extra-low housing prices that can seem like a bargain for a flipper looking to scoop up properties. But when those attractive prices are due to a negative catalyst, you can get stuck with inventory that simply won't sell. If any area suddenly undergoes a seismic shift in home sales, look to see if any of these reasons were behind the change:

- A major local employer is shutting down
- A sharp rise in crime rates
- Increased flooding

When you're looking at individual houses and not whole areas (especially if you're doing your flip shopping online), you may miss the bigger picture, and end up stuck with a home in an area that people are fleeing.

SECURE THE BEST FINANCING

Go for the Gold

When it comes to profitable house flipping, the best financing is your own cash. To be successful, you'll need plenty of it to cover the down payment and the renovations without getting buried in debt. Trouble crops up when those renovations cost more than anticipated, or when the house takes longer to sell than expected; either of those situations can tank an investment that's backed mainly by credit, especially if that credit comes with a high interest rate.

If you don't have quite enough cash to cover the purchase and the fix-up costs, you'll need to get a loan—but it's not like getting a loan for a house you're buying to live in. Many traditional lenders will not finance flips (especially first-timers) at all, and when they do, going this route can come with big drawbacks. Other cash sources include private lenders, hard money loans, and crowdfunding. Whichever path you decide to take to finance your flip, make sure you know exactly what you're getting into.

CASH IS KING

A lot of new real estate investors land in financial quicksand by purchasing a property for very little money down and relying on credit cards to fund repairs and renovations. If you want to improve your chances of success, build up a sizable cash balance before you begin flipping properties. Not only will that give you much more flexibility should things not progress as expected, it can also make it easier to get loans when you want them.

At Least 20 Percent Down

Because house flipping is a riskier proposition than a standard home mortgage, many traditional lenders (where you can get the best rates and loan terms) require at least a 20 percent down payment. Some lenders will ask for less, but it's in your best interests to put down as much as possible while still holding enough cash to cover the bulk of the renovations. Hitting that 20 percent mark gets rid of the PMI (private mortgage insurance) requirement, which can add up to 5 percent more to every loan payment.

Plus, the more money you put down, the less interest you'll pay over the life of the loan. In fact, a bigger down payment can often help secure a lower interest rate, decreasing expenses even further and building equity faster.

100 Percent Cash

The most successful flippers avoid loans all together and stick with straight cash to fund their investments. This strategy dramatically lowers the risk of loss, lowers the break-even point by minimizing expenses, and offers bigger profit potential. On top of that, avoiding a mortgage also means avoiding all the closing costs associated with a loan, which usually run close to 5 percent of the purchase price. On a $200,000 house, that would be an extra $10,000.

Repairs and renovations to your flip property could cost tens of thousands of dollars. If you use debt to pay for that, you'll end up paying thousands more in interest. Construction loans typically come with higher interest rates than mortgages, and funding repairs with credit cards bumps interest charges even higher. With healthy cash reserves, you won't be forced to fund renovations with credit cards or costly contractor loans.

Finally, sticking with cash helps you on the sales side too. If the house doesn't sell right away, you won't be stuck making mortgage payments while you wait for a buyer, and you won't feel pressured to keep dropping the price so you can pay off the loan.

Yes, it takes time to build up substantial enough cash reserves, and it's not an easy task. But if you're serious about making money by flipping houses, it's the most profit-friendly option.

TRADITIONAL LENDERS

Chances are, if you've ever had a mortgage, you've gotten it from a traditional lender like a bank or a credit union. Those loans are their bread and butter, and they love to close mortgages—but mainly for homes in move-in ready condition, the opposite of a fix-and-flip.

Choose the Best Mortgage

Be aware that many lenders won't work with first-time flippers, so without a successful track record, it may be hard to get a loan at all. You may be able to counteract their hesitance with a sizeable cash down payment and an excellent credit score. Partnering with an experienced contractor for renovations may also convince the lender to take a chance on you. Or you may have to find a more risk-friendly lender that will likely charge a high interest rate and higher loan fees, which will eat even further into your profits.

Be Aware of the Drawbacks

Most people feel comfortable going the traditional lending route because it's familiar, but using this financing for your flip can put you at a disadvantage. Drawbacks of traditional lending include:

- **Extended closing time.** Most traditional loans take at least thirty days (and some up to ninety days) to close, a definite drawback for a fix-and-flip investment.
- **Income requirements.** Traditional lenders want to see reliable income, especially for inexperienced flippers; that means W-2 income and steady paychecks—exactly what some people enter real estate investing to avoid.
- **Hard LTV.** Traditional lenders look at *current* appraisals to calculate the LTV (loan-to-value ratio), which they like to keep under 80 percent; that's a bad deal for a flipper who's scooping up *undervalued* properties because it could limit the loan amount.

That last point is one of the main reasons flippers avoid traditional lenders. They need loans to cover the purchase and the renovations. With a low appraisal value, it's nearly impossible to get a big enough loan to accomplish both. For example, say you want to buy a $200,000 house that needs renovations estimated at $40,000. If you have $50,000 to put down, you'd need to borrow $190,000. But to achieve an 80 percent LTV, the bank offers only a $160,000 loan—even though the house will be worth more than $240,000 after you've fixed it up.

The Lowdown on LTV

The LTV, or loan-to-value ratio, compares the loan amount to the current market value of the property. Banks use this number to determine risk. Lower LTV equals less risk, so a higher LTV can make it harder to get approved and harder to get a favorable interest rate.

PRIVATE LENDERS

Borrowing money from private lenders eliminates all the hassles of working with traditional lenders, but the convenience comes at a price. Basically, these are people with money to invest, and they're investing in your home flip; the interest you'll pay is their investment return, so it's in their interest to charge the highest possible rate. That means you'll have to sharpen your negotiating skills, because it's in your best interest to score the lowest possible interest rate on your flip loan.

Private lenders can come from your existing circle (a cousin who wants to invest in real estate without doing any of the hands-on work, for example), through a real estate agent you're working with to find flip properties, or by word of mouth from another real estate investor. Once you find your lender, the process moves at lightning speed compared to a traditional loan, closing in just a few days rather than in a month or two. Be prepared to hit the ground running.

Network and Negotiate

Newbie flippers need to find networking events where they can connect with more experienced flippers who've worked with private lenders. These invaluable connections offer multiple benefits, including introductions to flip-friendly private lenders, the inside scoop on fair interest rates, and learning how to walk away from a bad deal (even if it's the only deal on the table).

A mentor can also help you sharpen your negotiating skills, a crucial component of your real estate investing success. As you develop more confidence, you'll be able to work out better deals, and find it easier to tell good deals from bad.

Private lenders also attend these real estate networking events, looking for new opportunities, so you may walk out with full funding for your next flip.

Typical Terms

Private loans work similarly to traditional loans in that they come with a specific loan amount, a preset interest rate, and a first-position lien on the property. And like with traditional lenders, interest rates set by private lenders can vary widely because they depend on the deal you negotiate.

First-Position Lien

A lien is a legal claim against property (real or personal) that's been used as collateral for a loan. When a lender has the first-position lien, the lender gets paid first if the collateral (in this case, the flip house) has to be sold. This can happen if you default on the loan (stop making payments).

Often these lenders will also charge points (upfront interest payments) to help lower their investment risk. Points are calculated as a percentage of the loan balance (one point equals 1 percent). For example, one point on a $100,000 loan would be $1,000 (1 percent of $100,000). A private lender might charge 10 percent interest plus one point; that point would be paid at closing, and the 10 percent would be paid over the life of the loan.

Profit-Sharing Deals

Some private lenders may be willing to front you seed money in exchange for a piece of the action, acting more like partners. In this situation, they'll charge significantly lower interest rates in exchange for a portion of the profits once you sell. Typically, this type of deal would be offered to an experienced flipper with a proven track record, but you may be able to find a private lender even if you're not yet a seasoned real estate investing pro.

This kind of deal is also common when your lender is a friend or family member. To keep things professional, make sure that you have an experienced lawyer draft your loan and profit-sharing agreement.

Online Private Lenders

While private lenders are normally people you know (sometimes even friends and family), there are some who set up shop online and cater to property flippers. Technically, these companies qualify as private lenders because they're privately owned, but they're not what most people first think of for private lending.

Because these lenders have a lot of volume (they make more loans), they can offer lower rates; specific loan terms (including rates) may vary by state. Typically, these loans are limited to investors with at least a five-flip track record, another reason online private lenders can afford to offer more competitive rates.

Over the past few years, a lot of newcomers have entered this arena—some of them scam artists—so look for reviews before you choose an online site rather than just searching for the lowest rates. Private fix-and-flip lending sites with positive track records include LendingOne (www.lendingone.com) and Anchor Loans (www.anchorloans.com).

HARD MONEY LENDERS

Hard money lenders, also known as asset-based lenders, focus more on your potential property than on your income and credit score. Like other types of lenders, these will secure a first lien on the property. Because they specialize in flip loans, they'll want to make sure the property is likely to sell quickly so they can get their money back fast.

With this intense focus on the property, hard money lenders may also overlook down payment issues (like a borrowed down payment, which would eliminate most other types of lenders), as long as you have a substantial amount to put down. They'll care more about your ability to do a successful flip, so loan terms are almost always better for experienced flippers than first-timers.

This is probably the easiest place to find a flip loan, but it's also one of the more expensive options.

Standard Terms

In general, hard money loans for flippers have to be paid back within one year, and charge relatively high interest rates (sometimes as high as 18 percent) and points. Here, though, the points are typically not paid at the loan closing but when the property is sold (one borrower benefit of hard money loans). These are often interest-only loans, which means you only make the interest portion of monthly payments, then pay back the principal in one lump sum when your flip property is sold. In some cases, though, flippers make no payments until the house is sold, and the interest simply accumulates and gets added to the loan balance.

Loan amounts are based on the after-renovation value (ARV) of the house rather than the current market value, which helps flippers secure enough cash to buy and renovate the property. So, for example, if the market value of the home you want to flip is $100,000, but its ARV is projected as $150,000, your loan would be based on $150,000 (with a traditional lender, it would be based on the current $100,000 value).

Pros and Cons

Working with a hard money lender comes with several advantages and a few drawbacks. On the pro side, financing your flip this way:

- Means quick approval based on the target property
- Gets you cash quickly (mainly due to a shorter application and verification process)
- Offers more flexibility (like interest-only or deferred payments)
- Lets you borrow money even if your credit's not stellar

With flip-tailored loan terms, hard money lenders may seem like a dream come true, but they do come with some drawbacks. For one thing, these loans tend to be expensive, and that eats into your potential profits so you'll have less cash available for your next flip. For another, they usually offer relatively low LTVs (loan-to-value ratios), often hovering around 50 percent to 70 percent of the after-renovation value, which can leave you short on funds.

How to Find a Hard Money Lender

Start your search for a hard money lender online—you're more likely to find a company willing to work with novice flippers. Many of these companies will also offer advice and support; after all it's in their interest for your renovation and sale to go smoothly.

Make sure to look at independent reviews to make sure the lender is legit. You can find an extensive listing of hard money lenders on the BiggerPockets website (www.biggerpockets.com). Hard money lenders with proven track records include Lima One Capital (https://limaone.com) and AMZA Capital (https://amzacapital.com).

CROWDFUNDING YOUR FLIP

Crowdfunding (also called "peer-to-peer lending") involves getting a little bit of money from a lot of people, and it's one of the fastest growing ways to finance direct real estate investment. But it's also a relatively new industry, and not without some bugs. Here, lenders are considered investors who expect a good return on their money in the form of interest. Because regular crowdfunding websites don't really work for flippers (the loan amounts usually top out at around $35,000), specialty sites have cropped up.

These companies typically only work with experienced house flippers, but novices may be able to secure funding this way in some circumstances (partnering with a proven contractor, for example).

The Process

To the surprise of many novice flippers, there's a formal application process to go through before you can borrow money through reputable crowdfunding sites. In some cases, it starts with a quick basic loan application, which can usually be filled out in minutes. Then an expert from the site will connect with you to discuss your project in more detail and see whether your plan fits well in their model.

If they approve you, you'll have to fill out more paperwork and await their due diligence findings (such as verifying that you and the property really exist, getting an appraisal, etc.). Once you've cleared their hoops, you're set to get funding. Some companies prefund your loan, then open it to investors; others work in the opposite way. Make sure you understand the process because the timing differences can make or break your deal.

Beware the Downside

As with loans from hard money lenders, crowdfunded loans tend to focus more on the property characteristics and potential than on your personal credit track record, which can help people with lower credit scores get financing. But there are several drawbacks to using this method to get your flip financing:

- Long time to closing, as you wait for the funds to be collected from individual investors
- No deal if your pitch can't attract enough investors to fund your loan
- Relatively high interest rates
- No (or limited) chance to negotiate loan terms

Since this is a relatively new funding choice, expect big changes in the industry and the entry of new companies as demand from flippers and investors continues to grow.

Crowdfunding Choices

There are two main crowdfunding sites that work specifically with fix-and-flippers. (There used to be a third big player, RealtyShares, but the company fell on difficult times and is closed for new loans.)

- **Patch of Land** (www.patchofland.com) has a fix-and-flip program for loans ranging from $50,000 to $3 million, up to 85 percent LTV of the property. These loans typically have twelve-month terms, and interest rates start at 8 percent.
- **Groundfloor** (www.groundfloor.us) acts like a hard money lender, with rates starting at 5.4 percent and going as high as 26 percent. House-flipping loan amounts range from $75,000 to $2 million, up to 70 percent of ARV, and may close within fifteen days. The company tends to work with more experienced flippers.

LOW COST, NO STRINGS

Cheap and Easy

Real estate isn't cheap, and that's especially true for profitable commercial properties. That makes it harder for average investors (who don't have millions of dollars to tie up for decades) to benefit from this extremely lucrative asset class with direct investment. Luckily, buying properties isn't the only way to profit from real estate investing, and there are several ways you can buy in without breaking your bank.

Even though you'll escape the drawbacks of property ownership (such as large cash outlays and illiquidity), you'll still get all the benefits: steady income stream, growth potential, and diversification to stabilize your portfolio.

UNDER $100

Contrary to enticing clickbait headlines, it takes thousands of dollars *at least* to start investing seriously in physical real estate, and that's on the low end. You need a down payment, closing costs, and at least some savings to cover unexpected repairs to buy a property, and it can take longer than expected to start getting a dime back on your investment. Plus, while you're waiting to make money, the property costs money to hold and maintain.

With indirect real estate investing, you can get started for $100 or less. You can buy one share of stock, one share of an ETF (exchange-traded fund), or even buy into mutual funds for a tiny fraction of the price you'd pay for any property—and with the chance for faster returns.

How They Stack Up

A team of economists analyzed the returns of asset classes in sixteen countries over a 145-year period (1870–2015). Over that time, real estate had average annual returns of 7.05 percent compared to 6.89 percent for stocks. The order flips when just looking at US numbers: real estate returned 6.0 percent compared to 8.4 percent for stocks. But when the researchers adjusted for risk, real estate was by far the best choice: lower risk plus high returns. (Source: *The Rate of Return of Everything 1870–2015*, National Bureau of Economic Research.)

Freedom and Liquidity

Buying and selling real estate takes time. Even a lightning-fast closing takes weeks, and it normally takes months for deals to close and money to change hands—and that's *if* you can sell the property.

Indirect real estate investing gives you full liquidity. You can sell shares any day the markets are open and have cash in hand by the next day.

Buying real estate also almost always involves debt—and that can leave you tied to an investment you no longer want. It can also increase your losses if a property's market value moves in the wrong direction. Investing in lower-cost assets removes that chain (debt) that can force you to hold an unprofitable property.

REAPING THE SAME REWARDS

The biggest benefits of owning real estate come from steady cash flows and asset appreciation (the property grows in value over time). But those cash flows depend on having constant, reliable tenants (when you're a landlord), and real estate appreciation can take years or decades (unless significant desirable renovations are made).

With basic indirect investments (stocks, ETFs, and mutual funds), you can secure cash flow by buying income-producing securities (such as dividend stocks). Growth can happen much faster, and disappear just as quickly, but over the long term these investments tend to appreciate dramatically—especially if you're careful about the specific investments you choose.

There is one distinct advantage direct property investment holds over the indirect method: regardless of cash flow or market value, owning real estate gives you a tangible asset that has innate value no matter what you could sell it for. A house still exists and can be lived in even if its market value goes to zero; these indirect investments only have worth if the market says they do.

Investment Cash Flows

If you're looking for incoming cash—a key benefit of real estate investing—stocks, ETFs, and mutual funds can provide it. The trick is to buy income-producing investments: stocks that pay regular dividends or funds that hold dividend-paying securities.

Many ETFs and mutual funds hold pools of REITs (real estate investment trusts), which are required to distribute at least 90 percent of their earnings (usually from rent receipts) to shareholders; the fund (which acts as the main shareholder) in turn passes those dividends straight through to investors. Basically, you get to collect a portion of the rent on dozens (or hundreds) of properties. That works out to less than the cash flow you'd get owning a rental property, but it's also free of the debt, expenses, and headaches associated with being a landlord.

Asset Appreciation

Appreciation, or growth, refers to increased market value over time: you can sell an asset (such as a property or a stock) for more than what you paid. Both equity investments (which include stocks, ETFs, and mutual funds) and real estate tend to appreciate over time. But that doesn't happen in a straight line.

If you've watched the stock market at all, you know that values swing wildly up and down. Real estate values can move up and down as well, but not as quickly—mainly because you can't sell them instantly on a whim. Indirect real estate investments move more like stocks, but they may also gain a little more stability, especially when they're ultimately backed by real property (like REIT funds).

To take full advantage of appreciation potential with equity investments, you need to make a plan and stick with it no matter what the market's doing. Selling when stock prices fall locks in your losses; holding on to solid investments and giving them a chance to rebound regardless of the overall market gives you the best chance to watch your wealth grow over time.

ACCESS TO DIFFERENT TYPES OF PROPERTIES

A Building Buffet

Investing in real estate through stocks and funds is like an all-access pass to the industry. With indirect real estate investments, you gain the opportunity to invest in a wide variety of properties and property types—including some that are usually out of reach for individual investors. Each type of property comes with its own risk, benefits, profit potential, and income stream. Owning a mix of property types adds diversity to your real estate holdings, which helps mitigate any downturns in specific real estate sectors.

For example, commercial properties don't work the same way as residential properties; they come with longer-term leases, have less turnover, and command higher rents, but it also takes a bigger cash outlay to get started. Plus, because commercial properties are normally larger, they have much higher upkeep costs and expenses. In addition, different types of commercial properties behave in very different ways from an investment perspective. Brick-and-mortar retail stores have different life cycles than warehouses and manufacturing plants, for example, and office buildings earn income differently than hospitals.

RESIDENTIAL PROPERTIES

Residential rental properties refer to places where people live, their homes (as opposed to long term–stay hotels, for example).

Because you're familiar with how residential properties work, this can be the most comfortable place to get started in real estate investing.

Most residential property funds invest in REITs (real estate investment trusts) that directly hold underlying properties. The REITs collect rent, pass it on to the fund, and the fund passes it through to you. Because each REIT owns many properties, and each fund owns many REITS, investing through the fund gives you instant diversification in the residential space. You'll essentially be holding dozens of properties of different types in a variety of geographical areas.

The residential property category includes:

- Single-family rental homes
- Multi-family rental properties (like duplexes)
- Garden apartment communities
- High-rise apartment buildings
- Student housing (like dorms and off-campus apartments)
- Retirement communities
- Senior cohousing communities

When Residential Goes Commercial

In the world of real estate, residential rental properties with five or more units are sometimes considered commercial rather than residential. Other times, the residential/commercial classification is based on who's leasing the space: families or companies.

COMMERCIAL PROPERTIES

One advantage commercial properties have over residential properties: long-term leases. That adds stability to the investment, as there's less tenant turnover (something both sides—landlords and tenants—want). Most long-term leases include what are known as "elevator clauses." This allows for regular rent increases during the term of the lease so that the rent keeps up with inflation. Tenants and landlords always know when an increase is coming and how much it will be, which assists in long-term planning.

There are many different types of commercial properties, and each comes with its own twists. With so many options to choose from, we'll focus on two of the strongest categories. You can invest in these through individual stocks, but for the biggest opportunities, go for commercial real estate funds.

Brick-and-Mortar Retail

The brick-and-mortar retail industry has taken a beating as e-tailers like Amazon have joined the shopping scene. The category may be down (we've all seen stores disappear and malls close), but millions of people still prefer to shop at stores. In fact, new stores keep opening, despite dismal news reports on the in-person shopping industry.

That's mainly because real-life shops offer a lot that e-tailers just can't. It involves sensory experience, human interaction, and a shopping experience you won't find online. In fact, as stores continue to attract more shoppers, many online outfits have opened their own physical stores to keep up.

The retail category includes:

- Strip malls
- Grocery stores
- Drugstores
- Big-box stores
- Shopping malls with anchor stores
- Outlet malls

Medical

Commercial medical properties cover the gamut from individual doctor's offices to cutting-edge medical centers. This sector is seeing a lot of growth as a good chunk of the population ages (think baby boomers) and uses more medical services. Even without that, though, everyone needs medical care at one time or another, regardless of what's going on in the economy (and sometimes more when the economy starts to tank). New medical facilities are in development all around the country, and demand continues to outpace supply (at least for the foreseeable future).

Medical properties include:

- Hospitals
- Outpatient surgery centers
- Dialysis centers
- Nursing homes
- Diagnostic centers (labs, MRI and ultrasound centers, etc.)
- Mental health facilities
- Rehab facilities
- Long-term care facilities

REAL ESTATE–RELATED STOCKS

Supply-Side Investing

Real estate investing can involve more than directly or indirectly buying properties. There's a lot that goes into real estate, from development to construction materials to mortgage lenders. Through the stock market, you can participate in every aspect of real estate, beyond physical properties. With a long-term outlook, the stock market provides solid returns, easily outpacing inflation. The trick is to pick solid companies with strong potential and stick with them even when the market seems to be going crazy.

Real Estate Stocks versus REITs

People use the terms *real estate stock* and *REIT* interchangeably, but they aren't the same. Buying a real estate–related stock means buying shares of a single company. Buying shares of a REIT (real estate investment trust—see Chapter 4) means buying a piece of a full property portfolio.

HOW TO EVALUATE INDIVIDUAL STOCKS

Buying stock means buying part of a company. You wouldn't buy a business without looking into it, and the same holds true for buying stock; that calls for a thorough background check (which is much easier to do than it sounds). Since your goal is to build a fortune, you want to pick real estate stocks that will get you there. That means looking for companies with both a solid track record and the potential for future growth.

Once you've found some companies that fit the bill, you'll want to see how their stock has been performing. Factors outside a company's performance can affect the stock price: scandals, good or bad press, or economic changes, for example. When the company's true value is greater than its stock price indicates, you've uncovered a bargain.

Go to the Source

To find reliable information about a company and its stock, you want to use trustworthy sources. Two of the best resources are EDGAR, a comprehensive corporate database created by the Securities and Exchange Commission (www.sec.gov/edgar), and Value Line (www.valueline.com), a website containing tons of data and analysis on thousands of stocks.

Looking Backward

Numbers tell a story, and for corporations, that story is told through their financial statements, which you can find easily online. The three main financial statements include:

- **Balance Sheet:** a listing of the company's assets, liabilities, and equity, which shows you what they own and what they owe on a specific date.
- **Statement of Profit and Loss (also called Income Statement):** a summary of the company's revenues (sales), costs, and expenses which lead to its profits (or losses) for a specific time period.
- **Statement of Cash Flows:** a detailed look at how money moved in (sources of cash, like sales or borrowing) and out of the company (like debt payments or dividends for shareholders).

By taking a look at these statements, you begin to form a clear picture of the company's performance. What you want to see is a company that owns more than it owes, that has strong revenues and profits, and that brings in more money from operations than from borrowing.

Looking Forward

While the past can tell you a lot about a company's strength, as an investor you're more interested in what comes next—how profitable they're likely to be in the future. To learn that, you'll want to find out things like:

- Their goals and plans
- New products or services in the pipeline
- What new markets they plan to enter
- How they're adjusting for economic changes

You can find that information plus a look back at the successes and challenges of the year before in the company's annual report. Be aware that a lot of what you're reading will be hype—they want to show the corporation in the best possible light. But inside all the beautiful pictures and upbeat language will be a true indicator of where the company is going next.

Follow the Trends

Companies don't exist only on the dates of their financial statements—a lot happens in between. You can track the company and its stock by looking at performance trends. Several websites track stock prices and other key data points in real time, offering extensive information about every stock on the market.

You can see how the stock price has performed over a variety of periods, the company's earnings per share (EPS), how earnings compare to the stock price (the P/E, or price-to-earnings ratio), historical dividend payments, and much more. All you need to reach this wealth of information is the corporation's ticker symbol (its abbreviated name).

Websites that offer this real time information include Yahoo! Finance (www.finance.yahoo.com), Morningstar (www.morningstar .com), and MarketWatch (www.marketwatch.com). Most (if not all) online brokers also carry this information, along with other tools to help you make your decision.

INDUSTRIES CONNECTED TO REAL ESTATE

Think about what goes into designing a neighborhood, building a warehouse district, maintaining an office park, furnishing a chain of hotels. All of those activities (and so many more) are connected to real estate. If you think, for example, that the smart money is in warehouses, you could also profit from everything that goes into buying, building, furnishing, leasing, and maintaining warehouses.

Buying stock in real estate–related industries adds another dimension of diversification to your real estate holdings. Profits come from dividends (which not all corporations pay every year) and growth (increased stock price), and there's more opportunity for both with a buy-and-hold investment approach.

Developers and Builders

There are no homes, hotels, or hospitals that haven't been planned, designed, and built. To do that successfully, it takes skilled, experienced developers and builders. Companies with the foresight to buy land in strategic areas, create efficient home designs, and balance supply with market demand may remain profitable (or at least lose less) even during economic downturns.

Publicly traded developers and builders include:

- Lennar Corporation (LEN), one of the largest homebuilders in the US
- D.R. Horton (DHI), another of the largest homebuilders in America
- Jacobs Engineering Group (JEC), an architecture, engineering, and construction company

Construction Materials and Supplies

Whether they cater to national builders, local renovators, or DIY home projects, the companies that sell construction supplies and materials are crucial to the real estate industry. This includes everything from lumber and drywall to nails and bolts to sinks and toilets...essential components of every building.

Publicly traded materials and supplies companies include:

- Home Depot (HD)
- Lowes (LOW)
- Builders FirstSource (BLDR)
- Ingersoll Rand (IR)

Furnishings

Every building needs furnishings. That includes basics like light fixtures and window blinds for virtually any kind of building, as well as furniture and décor in office buildings and hotels. It also includes the linens, towels, and little touches that help make a house feel like a home.

Even when real estate sales are slowing down (and sometimes especially then), buildings still need furnishings. When people or companies can't afford to move, they may redecorate. When furniture and fixtures wear out, they need to be replaced.

Publicly traded home and office furnishing companies include:

- Williams Sonoma (WSM), a home furnishing conglomerate that holds a bunch of subsidiaries including Pottery Barn and West Elm
- Wayfair (W), which owns home furnishing brands like Joss & Main, Birch Lane, and AllModern
- Steelcase (SCS), the world's largest office furniture manufacturer

Real Estate Services

There are a few different types of real estate services corporations. Some are overarching support companies that take care of everything from property management to maintenance to janitorial services. Others are online real estate database services that hold easily accessible listings of commercial and residential properties.

Publicly traded corporations in this industry include:

- Cushman & Wakefield (CWK), a commercial real estate services company
- CBRE Group (CBRE), a global commercial and residential real estate services company
- Zillow Group (Z), an online real estate information company

REAL ESTATE MUTUAL FUNDS

A Big Basket of Buildings

Mutual funds first came on the scene in the 1920s, and they opened up a whole new world for individual investors. They work by pooling money from many investors and using that money to buy dozens (sometimes hundreds) of individual investments. That gives each investor a piece of all the holdings in the fund, rather than a piece of a single security. By offering instant and broad diversification, mutual funds help offset some of the risk inherent in investing. The same holds true for real estate mutual funds: they give you the opportunity to invest in a big basket of real estate investments for the price of a single share.

HOW MUTUAL FUNDS WORK

It's hard for individuals to buy a wide enough range of securities (such as stocks, bonds, or REITs) to diversify their portfolios and reduce their risk of total losses. Mutual funds solve that problem by using money from many investors to buy large baskets of different securities. Basically, by investing in a mutual fund, you own a piece of the whole portfolio for the same buy-in as if you'd bought one or two different real estate stocks.

Mutual funds come with their own lingo and a unique variety of expenses that can impact overall returns. To make smart choices, it's important to fully understand all the costs associated with buying fund shares; you should also look into securities the fund is holding.

There are two main ways to sort mutual funds: open-end versus closed-end and managed versus index. The main difference between open- and closed-end is the way they're traded. That can make a big difference when it comes to buying and selling shares. The key difference between managed and index funds is the way they choose holdings, which affects fund expenses and returns.

Open-End Funds

Open-end mutual funds are the kind most people are familiar with, where you buy or redeem (sell back) shares directly to or from the company. With open-end funds, the mutual fund company can issue as many shares as it wants. When you buy shares, the fund company creates them for you; when you redeem shares (sell them back), they vanish.

Since open-end funds don't trade over exchanges, the price is only published once a day, at the end of the day, by the mutual fund company. That price is based on the net asset value (NAV)—the total value of the mutual fund at that time. Because of their fee structures, mutual fund shares work best for long-term investors.

Closed-End Funds

Closed-end funds, or CEFs, seem the same as open-end funds, but they work quite differently. Though many people think the *closed* means these funds are closed to investors, it actually means that no more shares will be issued. CEFs work a little more like stocks. They're launched through IPOs (initial public offerings) with a fixed number of shares, and then those shares get traded on the open market over exchanges. Because they're publicly traded, the price may not be the same as the NAV; if the trading price is lower, that means shares are trading at a discount—the fund's holdings are worth more than the price suggests.

Another key difference: CEFs can use leverage (borrowed money) to try and produce higher returns. That strategy often pans out, but it also adds a layer of risk that open-end funds don't bear.

Managed Funds versus Index Funds

The other big chasm in the mutual fund world separates managed funds and index funds.

Managed funds have active fund managers, people who choose the securities the fund will hold. They aim to beat the market through strategic trading, offering the hope of substantially higher returns. That can increase turnover (how often securities are bought and sold), which can eat into returns. Because selecting the best holdings takes a lot of work, managed funds charge higher fees, which also reduce overall returns. For these funds, the management team is key; don't buy a managed fund without checking into the track record of the people making the choices.

What's an Index?

In investing, an index is an unmanaged group of securities used to measure market performance. It can be a measure of the market as a whole (like the S&P 500) or a particular sector (like the FTSE Nareit All Equity REITs Index). These indexes can be used as a fund's portfolio model or as a benchmark to measure returns against.

Index funds are passively managed. Their holdings track a designated benchmark index (like the S&P 500, for example). That means the fund holds the same securities as the index, usually in the same proportions. Since they don't have to pay a team of professionals to choose securities, index funds are able to charge ultra-low fees.

BUYING REAL ESTATE MUTUAL FUNDS

Once you've decided to invest in real estate mutual funds, you have two more big steps to take: choosing the funds and buying them. With dozens of funds to choose from, it helps to start with a plan. For example, do you want to stick with a low-cost index fund or take a gamble on potentially higher returns with a managed fund? Other factors that might drive your decision could include things like whether you want to invest in US or international real estate, or if you want a REIT-focused fund rather than a pure stock fund.

Examples of Real Estate Mutual Funds

There are two main ways mutual funds can invest in real estate: snapping up real estate–related stocks or buying REIT (real estate investment trust, covered in Chapter 4) shares, and some funds invest in a combination of the two.

Examples of real estate mutual funds include:

- **Fidelity Real Estate Investment Portfolio (FRESX),** a managed fund (so expect a higher expense ratio) that selects REITs with high-quality properties (mainly commercial and industrial)
- **Cohen & Steers Realty Shares (CSRSX),** a managed fund that holds a targeted portfolio of forty to sixty commercial REITs

- **Vanguard Real Estate Index Fund Admiral Shares (VGSLX),** a low-cost index fund that tracks a key REIT benchmark index (called the MSCI US Investable Market Real Estate 25/50 Index)
- **Cohen & Steers Quality Income Realty Fund (RQI),** a closed-end fund that holds a variety of high-income-producing commercial REITs and real estate–related stocks

Choosing the Right Fund

Before choosing a real estate mutual fund to invest in, you'll want to know what's in its portfolio. At least 80 percent of a fund's holdings have to be the investment type indicated by its name, but sometimes the names are (purposely) vague, allowing more flexibility. Make sure that the funds you consider actually contain the type of real estate investments you want.

You can narrow down potential picks using online fund screeners, available on sites like Morningstar (www.morningstar.com) and Kiplinger (www.kiplinger.com; click on the "Tools" section). If you already have a brokerage account, you'll have access to all of their screening tools as well.

Some of the factors to compare include:

- **Loads** are sales charges that kick in when you buy (front-end load) or sell (back-end load) open-end mutual fund shares.
- **Expense ratio** refers to ongoing fees for the fund, which range from 0.09 percent to more than 3 percent; lower fees are associated with index funds, higher fees with managed funds.
- **Minimum investment requirement** for open-end funds typically ranges from $500 to $3,000 for the initial investment only.
- **NAV (net asset value)** equals the total current value of all assets held by the fund minus any outstanding liabilities divided by the total number of outstanding shares [(assets – liabilities)/shares].

How to Buy and Sell Shares

Open-end mutual funds trade only at the end of the day based on their NAV (net asset value), and they can only be bought from the fund company itself. You can either go directly to the fund company to buy or buy funds through your own brokerage account (not all funds will be available through all brokers). For example, if you wanted to buy shares in a Fidelity real estate mutual fund, you could go to the Fidelity website (www.fidelity.com) or log in to your brokerage account (at TD Ameritrade or Charles Schwab, for example).

Closed-end funds (CEFs) trade directly over regular exchanges, just like stocks. They can be bought or sold any time of the day for the current price. Unlike open-end funds, CEFs trade at current market value, regardless of NAV.

REAL ESTATE ETFS (EXCHANGE-TRADED FUNDS)

Bundling Buildings

Exchange-traded funds (ETFs) have been around for a little more than twenty-five years, and they've had an explosive impact on individual investing. Because they're more transparent and less costly than mutual funds, ETFs have quickly grown in popularity, now holding more than $1 trillion in assets.

Because they're traded over exchanges, you have much more flexibility buying ETFs than traditional (open-end) mutual funds. And while they may seem like the same thing as CEFs (closed-end funds, a less common type of mutual fund), they're not; the only real similarities are that they're funds that trade over exchanges.

HOW ETFS WORK

Most exchange-traded funds are index funds. They look like index mutual funds from a distance, but they come with some important differences that benefit investors. Like index mutual funds, ETFs hold a wide variety of underlying investments (fifty different REITs, for example), offering instant diversification that's beyond the reach of most shareholders. Each share of the ETF owns a fraction of each of the underlying investments; so when you buy one share of an ETF, you're actually buying a portion of every one of its holdings (so you'd own a fractional share of fifty different REITs, for example).

The main way ETFs differ from mutual funds is in how they're traded. As the name spells out, ETF shares are traded over stock exchanges rather than bought (or sold) directly from (or to) the fund company. That gives you more flexibility and more control over your holdings, because you can trade ETFs at any time at the current market value.

Other important benefits include:

- **Ultra-low minimum investment.** You can buy a single share of an ETF (though that may not be cost effective due to trading fees).
- **No-commission trades.** Many brokers offer at least some ETFs that you can trade without paying brokerage fees.
- **Lower expense ratios.** Most ETFs are passive index funds and are able to charge very low expense ratios.
- **Liquidity.** You can buy or sell shares at any time without delay.
- **Transparency.** ETF portfolios mimic their benchmark indices, so you always know exactly which securities they're holding.
- **Tax advantages.** Since ETFs are passive funds, holdings are bought and sold infrequently, limiting capital gains that are passed through to investors.

On the con side, trading most ETFs will involve commissions, and those can eat into your profits, especially if you trade frequently.

BUYING REAL ESTATE ETFS

There are dozens of real estate ETFs and virtually all of them hold a variety of REITs (real estate investment trusts, discussed more in Chapter 4). When you buy these ETFs, you get instant access to huge, lucrative commercial properties like office complexes, high-rise apartment buildings, medical centers, manufacturing plants, and productive farmland. For the amount of money you'd need to put as a down payment on a house to rent (say $5,000), you could have an ownership stake in thousands of different properties through an REIT ETF.

REIT Indexes

There are dozens of indexes that track REITs, but only a few that are well known to investors. The two real estate indexes most commonly tracked by ETFs are MSCI US REIT Index and the Dow Jones US Select REIT Index. Both are very broad market indexes, covering a universe of publicly traded REITs. For information about other, more targeted REIT benchmarks, visit the National Association of Real Estate Investment Trusts (Nareit) at www.reit.com.

A Quick Look at REITs

REITs are special investment companies that own, manage, or finance large portfolios of properties. There are two main categories of REITs: equity and debt. Equity REITs are on the owning and managing property side, and they make most of their money from rent receipts and property appreciation. Debt REITs focus on the financing side, holding mortgages or mortgage-backed securities.

To qualify as a REIT:

- At least 75 percent of the company's assets have to be invested in real estate.
- At least 75 percent of its income has to come from real estate.
- At least 90 percent of its earnings have to paid out to investors.

Investing in REITs gives you access to large commercial properties and other real estate projects normally out of reach for individual investors. Though technically most publicly traded REITs don't have state minimum investment requirements, shares are often sold in blocks (which means you may have to buy ten or thirty shares at one time). Private and unlisted REITs do usually have very high minimum investment requirements, putting them out of reach for beginning investors—unless you buy into them through ETFs.

Choosing Real Estate ETFs

Like most other investment types (stocks or bonds, for example), REITs are tracked by a variety of indexes. REIT ETFs passively track those indexes, which means they hold all of the REITs included in the index (sort of like a copy). Because these funds are just following the index, their expense ratios are extremely low, which means you get higher returns on your investment.

REIT ETFs can cover a broad market (like all equity REITs) or a narrow slice (like hotel REITs). Examples of real estate ETFs include:

- **Vanguard Real Estate ETF (VNQ),** which follows the MSCI US Investable Market Real Estate 25/50 Index (a broad REIT index)
- **iShares Global REIT (REET),** which tracks the FTSE EPRA/ NAREIT Global REIT Index and holds a combination of US and overseas property REITs
- **Pacer Benchmark Industrial Real Estate Sector ETF (INDS),** a targeted fund that follows the Benchmark Industrial Real Estate SCTR Index with an emphasis on industrial (such as cell towers and data centers) and self-storage properties
- **Schwab US REIT ETF (SCHH),** which tracks the Dow Jones US Select REIT Index, holding a broad mix of residential and commercial REITs

USING A BROKERAGE ACCOUNT

Buy Low, Sell High

All of these indirect real estate investments call for a brokerage account, a special investment account that lets you buy and sell a wide variety of securities, including stocks, bonds, mutual funds, and ETFs. When you're first getting started, using a brokerage firm that offers a lot of support and educational materials will serve you better than one geared toward experienced traders.

The right platform can help you build a more stable, more profitable portfolio as you learn the ins and outs of investing. And as you get more experienced, you'll be able to take advantage of more sophisticated trading features.

CHOOSING YOUR BROKERAGE

Before you pick a brokerage company, you'll need to decide on the level of service you want. Brokerage account options run from automated robo-advisors to DIY setups to on-demand face-to-face access. Whichever is the most comfortable for you is the best place to start; you can always change if it doesn't work out for you.

When you're new to investing, you'll need access to educational content (even if you're using a full-service financial advisor) because it's crucial to understand your investments and how they fit into your overall portfolio. You'll also want easy access to screening and sorting tools to help you narrow down the thousands of investment choices available to you.

Online Broker

Online brokerage companies are great for people who are comfortable doing their own research and executing their own trades. Taking the DIY approach cuts down on fees, which is why these are also often called discount brokers. They also offer low or no minimum investment requirements, so you can start buying shares without shelling out thousands.

The best online brokers provide free selection tools (like stock and fund screeners), investment research, educational content, and trading tutorials. Fees and commissions should be clearly spelled out, along with minimum investment requirements, so you won't have surprises on your monthly statements. Many online brokers offer access to no-fee ETFs and mutual funds, and charge relatively low trading fees for individual stocks. They also offer secure apps so you can track your investments on the go.

Solid online brokers include E-Trade (www.etrade.com) and Ally Invest (www.ally.com/invest).

Should You Go Robo?

Robo-advisors use complex algorithms to choose investments for you based on your answers to a series of questions. These programs are very cost-efficient, but their investment options can be limited. While robo-advisors are excellent for general stock investing, they're not the best choice for real estate investing.

Full-Service Brokers

Full-service brokerage firms offer top-of-the-line attention to your portfolio for a fee. You'll connect with a dedicated advisor who will get to know you and your financial goals and then choose investments for you to help you meet those goals. They do all of the legwork and the trading—and that level of service isn't cheap. Full-service brokers may charge a percentage of the assets they have under management, commissions on trades, and may also earn commissions for steering you toward specific investments. Working with a fee-only or fiduciary broker can help ensure that both of you are working in your best interests.

While a full-service broker may seem like overkill for choosing and trading stocks, ETFs, and mutual funds, this kind of broker offers a lot of benefit when you're ready to turn toward more sophisticated real estate investments (covered in Chapter 4). Even if you're not interested in working with one of these pricier advisors now, start looking into them to see which best align with your plans and values. That way when you are ready to take real estate investing to the next level, you'll know which direction to head.

Full-service brokers include Merrill Lynch (www.ml.com), Ameriprise Financial (www.ameriprise.com), and Edward Jones (www.edwardjones.com).

Hybrid Brokers

Many financial service firms offer combined services: online investment platforms (DIY or robo) with input from financial advisors when you want it. These brokerage companies start with a digital analysis of your cash balances and existing investment portfolio. Next, you talk with a financial planner (usually by phone or Skype, but sometimes in person) about your life goals and together come up with an investment strategy to get you there.

These companies generally charge more than straight online brokers but still considerably less than full-service brokers. You'll likely be charged one fee for your DIY trades and another when working with an advisor. Another difference, you may not have a dedicated financial advisor—you'll probably talk with whoever happens to be available when you need help.

Hybrid brokerage firms include:

- TD Ameritrade (www.tdameritrade.com) offers online DIY trading and has fully staffed offices throughout the US so you can meet with an advisor face-to-face.
- Charles Schwab (www.schwab.com) has a robust robo-platform, self-directed online trading, and advisors you can talk with or meet with as needed.
- Fidelity (www.fidelity.com) offers 24/7 live investment assistance along with their online trading services.

All three of these hybrid brokerages (along with most others) offer secure apps that let you move money, trade shares, and keep up with investment performance no matter where you are.

REGULAR OR RETIREMENT ACCOUNT?

Another factor to consider as you begin investing in real estate is whether you want to hold those investments in regular brokerage accounts or retirement accounts. Each type has benefits and drawbacks, and most people do best with a combination of both.

Regular Taxable Account

With a regular taxable account, you will pay tax on earnings and capital gains every year (capital losses will reduce your tax bill). Interest and dividend earnings get taxed in the year you *earn* them, whether or not you take them as cash (rather than reinvesting them). Capital gains (and losses) only come into play when you sell an investment; you don't have to pay any tax on asset appreciation as long as you hold on to the asset.

The plus side of this current taxation is flexibility and accessibility. Regular accounts have no restrictions on putting money in or taking it out (other than any specific brokerage restrictions regarding minimum balances or maximum number of withdrawals). You can access your money for any reason at any time without fear of tax penalties. And if you want to reduce your taxable income, you can sell a losing investment for a capital loss; that loss offsets other income to lower your tax bill, which can be a useful tax strategy. The same transaction inside a retirement account wouldn't have any current tax impact.

Retirement Account Options

Real estate investments work well as long-term holdings, and that makes a solid choice for retirement accounts. This is money that will be locked away, inaccessible (without big penalties) until you're at least fifty-nine-and-a-half years old. In exchange, you won't have to pay any taxes on any earnings inside the account until you eventually take the money out.

When your money grows tax-deferred (and, in some cases, tax-free), it grows faster due to the power of compounding. Annual taxes chip away at your portfolio balance, so an account where that doesn't happen will naturally accumulate more money over time.

Virtually all brokerage firms offer individual retirement accounts (IRAs). There are two main types: traditional and Roth. The main difference between them is tax treatment. Traditional IRAs give you a tax deduction now, and tax-deferred growth for the money in the account; you pay taxes only when you begin to withdraw money. Roth IRAs give you no tax deduction now, but all of the money in the account grows *tax-free* as long as you don't take it out early (the after-tax money you put in you can still access penalty-free if you need to).

Compounding Grows Your Money

Compounding is a process where your money earns more money for you. Say you invest $100 and it earns $3 in returns. Next year, you have $103 invested and earning. Those earnings accumulate over time at an accelerated rate because your earnings are now also earning on their own.

Setting Up Your Account

It takes about ten to fifteen minutes to set up an online brokerage account. When you're ready to set up yours, you'll need to have some basic information handy:

- Full contact information
- Social Security number
- Driver's license
- Regular bank routing and account numbers

Once the account is open, you'll need to fund it with a deposit check or a direct transfer from your bank (much faster and easier). Depending on which method you choose, it can take anywhere from three business days to a week for the funds to show up in your account. Once they're, you're ready to buy your first investment.

If you're working with a full-service broker, the setup takes longer because together you'll need to map out your goals and plans and take your whole financial picture into account. This can take an hour or two—but they do most of the work for you.

CHAPTER 4

REI ON THE SIDE— THE NEXT LEVEL

When you're ready to take real estate investing a step further, you'll enter a world of more complex and potentially more profitable investment choices. Most of these investments require bigger cash infusions than other indirect property investments, and it can be much harder to sell or redeem your holdings than it is with more traditional investments.

Be aware that the investments in this chapter can get complicated. When you're just starting out in this arena, it's best to work with an experienced advisor.

CHOOSING A NEXT-LEVEL FINANCIAL ADVISOR

You Have to Know a Guy

Many financial advisors fall short when it comes to expanding into real estate–based investments. While they may know a bit about publicly traded REITs (real estate investment trusts), their knowledge about nonlisted real estate investments, which include limited partnerships, interval funds, and other private opportunities, could be limited. Without in-depth expertise in the real estate industry and these next-level investments, these financial professionals won't be able to advise you properly about the more sophisticated ways to include real estate in your portfolio.

A Word About Opportunity Cost

Opportunity cost refers to the investments you can't make because of the investment you did choose; in other words, a trade-off. Because high-level real estate investment usually requires a relatively large amount of cash, the opportunity cost can be higher than with other investments.

That's why it's critical to find an advisor with the right experience. The best way to do that is by asking questions until you find an advisor that you like and feel comfortable with and that also has a solid background in real estate investing.

WHAT A FINANCIAL ADVISOR DOES

Financial advisor is an umbrella term used to describe professionals who can assist with investing, financial planning, and asset management. When you first start working with a financial advisor, expect to answer a lot of questions (if they don't ask questions, find someone else) about your current financial situation, risk tolerance, and goals. Your advisor may also talk with you about tax planning (to help you keep as much of your investment profits as possible), estate planning (which can include life insurance and trusts), and education planning (if you have children who may attend private school or college).

Some financial advisors will meet with you a few times, help you develop a plan, leave you in the driver's seat, and then check in with you periodically to make sure your plan is on track. Others take a more intensive approach, which may include asset management (he or she makes investment decisions for you based on your plan). Once you've decided which approach feels more comfortable for you, you can start looking for an advisor that fits your needs. To get involved in high-level real estate investing, make sure the advisor you choose understands the industry.

Use FINRA

The Financial Industry Regulatory Authority (FINRA) is a great resource for learning more about the different types of financial advisors and recommended qualifications. They also offer a free BrokerCheck tool so you can verify licenses and credentials. Visit their website at www.finra.org.

Traditional Financial Advisors Don't Recommend Real Estate

Most financial advisors trade in stocks, bonds, mutual funds, and occasionally REITs. That's because many financial advisors get paid brokerage commissions based on which investments you buy, and they won't get that commission if they recommend direct real estate holdings (unless they're also licensed real estate agents). But even fee-based financial advisors won't normally know much about real estate investing beyond REITs (and many don't really understand the ins and outs of REIT investing, either), because that's just not part of what they're normally taught.

Wealth Management

While asset management focuses strictly on portfolio assets, wealth management takes a broader, whole-person/family approach. Services under a wealth manager could include tax and estate planning, charitable giving (through a family foundation, for example), and asset protection.

There are financial advisors that do specialize in real estate, but you'll probably have to dig around to find them. This is where networking can come in handy—the best advisors get clients through recommendations, so ask other real estate investors you know and trust who they're working with.

Asset Management

When you've built up a sizeable fortune, professional asset management can help you make the most of your wealth. Basically, you hand over a large sum of money and the management company invests it according to your life plans and financial goals, with the intent of maximizing your nest egg. Working with an asset manager gives you access to private and alternative investments that aren't available to the general public (like private real estate funds and nonlisted securities).

Typically, asset managers get paid a percentage of the total holdings under their management. As the portfolio grows, the percentage usually decreases (though the actual dollar amount of the fee increases).

Integrated Asset Management

There's a relatively new form of financial planning that's been picking up steam for the past couple of years: integrated asset management (IAM). Unlike traditional financial planners that focus on stocks and bonds, these firms cover a broader range of asset types and include experts in real estate investing and development. By combining these types of expertise, IAMs are better able to help real estate investors create profitable, well-diversified portfolios and connect them with high-level real estate investment opportunities.

FIND A FIDUCIARY

No matter what type of financial advisor you decide to work with, you want to choose a *fiduciary*. Fiduciaries are legally and ethically obligated to put your interests ahead of their own, and they're required to avoid any conflicts of interest. That means they cannot encourage you to invest in deals that they (or people close to them) will profit from personally. It also means they're held to a higher standard where due diligence is concerned, an important factor in high-level investing.

Fee-Based Is Better

To avoid one area of conflict, fiduciary financial advisors work for fee-based rather than commission-based compensation. They get paid the same amount regardless of what you invest in or how often you buy or sell securities. That setup removes the temptation to steer clients toward investments or trading activities that will line their own pockets.

Brokers and product salesmen count on commissions; they get paid more when you buy specific investments. That gives them incentive to sell you products rather than look for the best investment options for your portfolio. When you add pricey real estate investments into the mix, unscrupulous advisors may lead you into bad deals to score big commissions for themselves.

Stick with a fee-based advisor (percentage-of-assets fees are not commissions) to make sure your advisor is working to build your wealth.

Know the Credentials

A lot of advisors have an alphabet soup of letters after their names, and it's important to know which of those initials really count when you're choosing your financial advisor. You want your advisor to have credentials that carry weight, that have to be earned with experience and education, not just a quick online quiz. And you want to know which credentials signify fiduciary responsibilities. Look for at least one of these credentials before you sign on with any financial advisor:

- AAMS (Accredited Asset Management Specialist)
- CFA (Chartered Financial Analyst)
- CFP (Certified Financial Planner)
- RIA (Registered Investment Advisor)
- CCIM (Certified Commercial Investment Member)

There are a lot of other initials floating around, but these all require a commitment to ethics as part of the certification.

EQUITY REITS (REAL ESTATE INVESTMENT TRUSTS)

Your Own Piece of the Pie

Equity REITs (pronounced "reets") give small investors the chance to get in on big investment opportunities without actually having to own any property. Every REIT pools money from investors to buy and hold investments somehow related to real estate, sort of the way mutual funds and exchange-traded funds (ETFs) pool money from investors to buy a wide variety of stocks or bonds. They earn income from various sources, though it's mainly from rental receipts.

Investing in REITs gives you an extra layer of diversification (which means holding many different asset types) if most of your investments are in the stock market (most people's are, especially retirement portfolios). Diversification helps reduce the overall risk factor of your portfolio. Plus, REITs often outperform the stock market, especially over long periods of time. That's because their total return includes a combination of income and growth.

REITS DEFINED

Unlike other types of investments, REITs have to follow a unique set of strict requirements to maintain their REIT status. That's true no matter what type of REIT you choose to invest in (and there are several distinct types) and whether it's publicly or privately traded.

To qualify as a REIT, the company must have at least one hundred investors. It also has to earn at least 75 percent of its income from real estate, which includes real estate–related sources such as mortgage loans. At least 75 percent of its assets have to be invested in real estate. But what really matters to investors is that every year, a REIT has to distribute 90 percent of its income directly to shareholders in the form of dividends. If you're looking for an investment that guarantees cash coming in, REITs by nature satisfy that goal.

REITs Are Big Business

According to the National Association of Real Estate Investment Trusts (Nareit), equity REITs hold more than two hundred thousand properties across the United States, and hold real estate assets valued at nearly $2 *trillion*.

If the company meets all of the qualifications for a REIT, it enjoys special tax status: it doesn't have to pay *any* taxes at the company level, which means more cash and higher returns for shareholders. (This is in contrast to the double-taxation issues of corporate stocks, where the corporation has to pay taxes on its income before distributing dividends to shareholders, and then the shareholders have to pay taxes on the dividends they receive, resulting in the same money being taxed twice.)

DIFFERENT TYPES OF EQUITY REITS

There are many different types of REITs, but at the top level they're first divided into public and private, which describes how people invest in them. Publicly traded REITs are traded on the stock exchange, just like regular stocks. This offers investors more liquidity (meaning they're easier to sell if you need to cash out). Nonlisted public REITs are available to the public but are not listed or traded on exchanges. Private REITs aren't available to the general public, so they're generally only accessible to individual investors through specialized advisors.

The next layer is divided between equity and debt REITs. Debt REITs focus on the loan side of the business, holding mortgages or mortgage-backed securities, so their earnings rely mainly on mortgage interest receipts (we'll talk more about these in the next section). Most REITs fall into the equity category (when people talk about REITs, this is usually what they're referring to), meaning they own, develop, and operate actual real estate assets (like office buildings, malls, and medical centers).

From there, equity REITs are classified mainly by the types of properties they specialize in, and that can be virtually any type of property you can think of: apartment buildings, self-storage facilities, warehouses, marinas, and more.

Retail REITs

REITs holding retail properties make up the biggest segment of equity REITs, coming in at around 17 percent. Some retail REITs hold a variety of property types, others focus on single types such as outlets, malls, or stand-alone stores. Those stores include everything from high-end department stores to supermarkets to big-box retailers.

You can easily buy shares in any of thirty-six publicly traded retail REITs, which offer yields topping 4 percent (on average). Examples of retail REITs include:

- Getty Realty Corp. (GTY), which holds convenience stores and gas stations and has a yield of 4.42 percent

- Four Corners Property Trust (FCPT), which holds more than five hundred restaurants in forty-four states and yields 4.18 percent
- SITE Centers Corp. (SITC), which holds shopping centers in major metropolitan areas around the US and has a yield of 6.40 percent

Residential REITs

A good-sized chunk of REITs (around 14 percent, according to Nareit) focuses on residential properties. This category includes things like apartment buildings, single- and multi-family rental properties, student housing, and senior housing (such as retirement communities and senior cohousing properties).

While these REITs may have lower yields than other categories, they tend to have lower risk profiles and high-growth potential (which increases total returns). Examples of residential REITs include:

- AvalonBay Communities (AVB), which holds apartment communities throughout the US and has a yield of 3.15 percent
- American Campus Communities (ACC), which holds student housing communities in the US and yields 4.25 percent
- Equity Lifestyle Properties (ELS), which holds manufactured home communities, campgrounds, and RV resorts in North America and has a yield of 2.19 percent

Healthcare REITs

There are eighteen publicly traded healthcare REITs, and these hold a variety of medical-related properties. While a few hold a broad range of real estate types, most healthcare REITs have a narrow focus, specializing in properties such as hospitals, senior living facilities, and medical office buildings. Average yields in this sector top 5 percent.

Examples of publicly traded healthcare REITs include:

- National Health Investors (NHI), which specializes in a variety of senior-related properties such as skilled nursing facilities and memory care facilities and has a yield of 5.01 percent.
- Medical Properties Trust (MPW), which holds properties including women's and children's hospitals and community hospitals and yields 5.90 percent.
- Physicians Realty Trust (DOC), which holds strategically located healthcare properties associated with hospitals or physician organizations and yields 5.25 percent.

Other Equity REIT Sectors

If you can imagine a type of property, there's a REIT that specializes in it. From tropical island resorts to state-of-the-art medical facilities to movie theaters, you can buy shares in any type of property that you want to and get guaranteed cash flow from your investment.

- Lodging REITs (e.g., Hospitality Properties Trust [HPT]), which hold properties such as hotels, resorts, and travel centers.
- Self-storage REITs (e.g., Public Storage [PSA]), which specialize in both owning self-storage facilities and renting storage spaces to customers.
- Office REITs (e.g., Boston Properties [BXP]), which own, operate, and lease space in office buildings.
- Industrial REITs (e.g., PS Business Parks [PSB]), which own and manage properties such as warehouses and distribution centers.

- Data center REITs (e.g., Equinix [EQIX]), which own data centers, properties that store and operate data servers and other computer networking equipment.
- Timberland REITs (e.g., Rayonier [RYN]), which hold forests and other types of real estate dedicated to harvesting timber.
- Specialty REITs, which narrow in on very specific properties such as casinos, cell phone towers, or educational facilities.

THE PROS AND CONS
OF INVESTING IN REITS

There's a reason REITs are popular among wealthier investors: they offer a lot of benefits with fewer risks than other common investment assets. With a solid history of steady, high returns, constant cash flow, and long-term appreciation potential, REITs make a strong addition to any portfolio. What makes them even better is their diversification factor, adding a new asset class into typically stock-heavy nest eggs. Of course, like all investments, equity REITs also come with some risks.

Access and Income

The main appeal of REITs is that they give regular people access to big-ticket deals. You can buy into a REIT for $5,000 (and sometimes as little as $500), but you couldn't take part in a $5 million commercial real estate deal without ten times more cash on hand.

Another key reason investors love REITs: they provide reliable income streams in the form of dividends, usually much higher than income from other fixed-income investments. Plus, because of the way they're structured, REITs offer steady cash flow even during economic slowdowns.

Investment Risks

REIT share prices are more sensitive to changes in interest rates than some other investment assets (like stocks). When interest rates rise, REIT prices begin to drop. The opposite holds true too: when rates go down, REIT share prices rise.

Just like millions of homeowners took a financial bath when real estate prices dropped dramatically when the housing bubble burst, REIT-held property values plummeted too. That dragged share prices down and even drove some of the more leveraged REITs (ones with a lot of debt) to the brink of bankruptcy. Also, a REIT that's carrying a lot of debt could be in financial trouble (just like a person buried in student loans and credit card debt) no matter how many profitable properties it holds. That's why it's important to carefully research any REIT you're thinking of buying into, the same way you would before buying any other investment.

You also have to consider property-specific risks. For example, a REIT that holds primarily retail properties (like stores, malls, and mini-malls) could be badly affected by retail bankruptcies (think Borders or Toys "R" Us) and mall closures, which are becoming more common due to the increase in e-tailers.

HOW TO INVEST IN EQUITY REITS

Most equity REITs are bought and sold over national exchanges, just like regular corporate stocks. In fact, more than eighty million

Americans invest in REITs, mainly through funds in their retirement accounts (though they may not realize it).

Just like with stocks, you can find up-to-the-minute data and detailed analysis on any publicly traded REIT. You'll look for information on its listing price, current yields, growth trends, management experience, and underlying asset values; you can find that information simply by doing an online search using the REIT's name or trading symbol.

Once you choose a REIT to invest in, contact your broker (whether it's a person or an online trading platform) and buy shares—it's that easy.

Nonlisted and Private REITs

Nonlisted public and private REITs are sold only through financial advisors rather than over exchanges, and investors have to meet minimum suitability requirements to buy in. Nonlisted public REITs must still register with the Securities and Exchange Commission and provide regular financial disclosures; private REITs do not.

Both come with higher investment minimums than publicly traded REITs. Nonlisted public REITs typically have minimum buy-ins of $1,000 to $2,500. Private REITs may require minimum investments in the $10,000 to $25,000 range.

The fact that these securities don't trade over a public exchange adds a lot of stability to the investment (share prices don't move with the whims of the market), but it comes at a price; these long-term investments are not liquid. Depending on the terms of the REIT, investments are typically locked in by minimum holding periods (often at least a few years) with redemption exit ramps starting after ten years. Most nonlisted REITs have occasional liquidity events, where they allow investors to redeem a portion of their holdings, but those may not coincide with your cash needs. While there is a secondary market (other investors you could sell to), it's not as big, and you might not be able to sell for as much as your holdings are actually worth.

Choosing Equity REITs

Once you're ready to invest in equity REITs, you'll start by choosing a sector (like healthcare or retail) to help you narrow down the options; after all, there are hundreds to choose from. After that, look at the list of REITs in that niche and do some research. Which you choose will depend on several factors, including your other holdings, risk tolerance, investment horizon (how long you plan to hold the REIT), and income needs.

Good sources of information about management, performance, and future growth potential include Nareit (www.reit.com), Morningstar (www.morningstar.com), and Yahoo! Finance (www.finance.yahoo.com).

It can help to loop in an experienced advisor to help you sort through the REIT choices, and figure out which would fit best into your overall financial plan.

MORTGAGE REITS

Cash In on Debt

Mortgage REITs invest in the other side of real estate: debt. They either invest in mortgages (through mortgage-backed securities), buy up existing mortgages, or act as direct mortgage lenders. These REITs earn their profits mainly through the interest generated on the loans they hold (directly or indirectly).

Mortgage REITs by the Numbers

There are forty-one publicly traded mortgage REITs (sometimes called mRE-ITs). They've helped finance 1.8 million homes in America, and thousands of commercial properties. You can find a comprehensive list of public (listed and nonlisted) mREITs at www.reit.com.

Though there are substantially fewer mortgage REITs than equity REITs, they draw high-level investor attention due to their high returns (some topping 10 percent) and steady cash payouts.

HOW MORTGAGE REITS WORK

Instead of holding a portfolio of properties, mortgage REITs count mortgage loans and mortgage-backed securities among their assets. Rather than rent receipts, mREITs bring in interest income that comes from payments made on the underlying mortgages. These

REITs usually pay higher dividends than equity REITs and also come with more downside risk.

Typically, mortgage REITs specialize in either residential or commercial mortgage debt, though a few hold both types. Some offer direct loans to finance property purchases or development projects. Others buy up existing mortgages, while some invest in agency mortgage-backed securities. Regardless of the type of debt they hold, all of it is backed by physical real estate.

Debt to Equity

Mortgage REITs are funded by a combination of equity (money from investors) and debt (money the REIT has borrowed) that's used to purchase the assets they hold. Their main goal: earn more interest on their holdings than they pay on their debt. That difference (between what they receive and what they pay) is called the "spread," and it's how mortgage REITs maintain profits and pay out income to investors.

When more of their holdings are financed by debt, that spread will be smaller, eating into investor earnings. To reduce risk, investors can focus on REITs with less leverage. According to Nareit (www.reit.com), the industry median leverage for mortgage REITs is 4×, meaning holdings are financed by four times more debt than equity. For example, with 4× leverage, a $1,000,000 holding would be backed by $200,000 equity and $800,000 debt; four times more debt than equity.

When Interest Rates Rise

Mortgage REITs tend to take price hits when interest rates rise, and that's especially true if rates increase quickly and unexpectedly. That's because their holdings bring in the old, lower rate, and investors want to earn the new higher rates. Again, this pricing issue really comes into play if you're trying to sell shares.

Often, mortgage REITs in this situation look to increase their overall returns gradually by adding new, higher-rate securities to their portfolios. That means bigger cash flows and higher returns for investors too. Therefore, holding on to a mortgage REIT and giving it a chance to adapt to interest rate changes can keep investors earning the highest possible returns.

COMMERCIAL VERSUS RESIDENTIAL

Mortgage REITs fall into two broad categories: commercial and residential. While both involve loans secured by property, they don't work in quite the same way. Commercial loans tend to have lower loan-to-value ratios (LTVs) than residential loans and shorter loan terms that end in balloon payments. Residential mortgages come with longer loan terms and higher LTVs.

LTV

LTV stands for "loan-to-value," a ratio that determines the maximum loan amount based on the value of the property. For example, if a property was worth $100,000 and the lender's maximum LTV was 75 percent, the borrower could not get more than $75,000 of financing.

Commercial mREITs tend to hold fewer, larger loans, as commercial real estate deals call for more financing. Conversely, residential mREITs may hold tens of thousands of individual home mortgages, whether by owning those debts directly or through mortgage-backed securities.

Commercial mREITs

Commercial mREITs create, buy, and invest in loans secured by commercial real estate. Commercial real estate loans tend to have short loan terms, five to twenty years, even though the loans might be amortized over thirty years; that results in a balloon payment (the full remaining loan balance) at the end of the loan term. In addition, commercial loans tend to have LTVs ranging from 65 percent to 80 percent, much lower than homeowner mortgage loans; that means the borrowers have to put up more capital in order to qualify for the loan, reducing the risk of default.

Though most hold a variety of commercial mortgages, the category also includes more specialized REITs that focus on a specific type of commercial real estate properties.

Examples of publicly traded commercial mREITs include:

- Jernigan Capital (JCAP), which specializes in self-storage facilities and has a 6.62 percent yield
- Apollo Commercial Real Estate Finance (ARI), which holds commercial real estate debt and has a yield of 9.86 percent
- Blackstone Mortgage Trust (BXMT), which originates loans backed by commercial properties in the US and Europe and has a yield of 7.15 percent

All of these (and more) are listed on public stock exchanges, making them easy to buy and sell (as long as you have a brokerage account). There are also nonlisted and private commercial mortgage REITs that you can access through a financial advisor.

Amortization

Amortization is a method used to calculate the principal and interest portions of payments on a mortgage loan based on the current loan balance. As the loan balance decreases, the interest portion shrinks and the principal portion grows. In partial payment situations, the interest portion always gets paid first.

Residential mREITs

Residential mREITs may hold either pools of mortgage loans or mortgage-backed securities (MBS, bonds backed by mortgages). Most focus their holdings on agency MBS (more on those later in this chapter), which have lower credit risk because they're backed or guaranteed by federal government entities. Still there is plenty of risk here, especially prepayment risk, which comes into play when homeowners sell or refinance their homes. When that happens, it permanently reduces the REIT's future income stream.

Publicly traded residential mREITs include:

- Ellington Residential Mortgage REIT, trading as EARN and yielding 12.30 percent
- Armour Residential REIT, trading as ARR and yielding 10.39 percent
- Capstead Mortgage Corporation, trading as CMO and yielding 6.64 percent

As with all investments, higher returns are associated with higher risk levels, so don't judge REITs based solely on their current yields.

REAL ESTATE INVESTMENT GROUPS

The In-Crowd

To directly participate in high-level real estate projects, some investors turn to real estate investment groups. Though it might sound like this is just a bunch of people getting together to buy real estate, that's not how these groups work. Rather, they're more like small mutual funds that hold one or more large rental properties and allow investors to buy pieces; for example, an investor could buy two apartments in a building.

This setup allows you to invest directly in real estate property without any of the headaches that come with being a landlord.

There are a few different types of setups that fall under this heading, but the two main types are basic real estate investment groups and real estate limited partnerships. Each works differently, but the premise is the same: you'd have a direct investment in a larger real estate holding than you could afford on your own.

Not a Club

Many people talk about real estate investment groups when what they're really referring to is investment clubs (discussed later in this chapter). These two vehicles are not the same: clubs are comprised of members who pool funds to buy properties according to group wishes; investors in groups have no vote, other than deciding whether or not to buy in.

In virtually all cases, you'd need to make these investments through an advisor, though some groups do offer direct investing. Enter these deals cautiously and only after you've performed due diligence on both the company and the investment property.

REAL ESTATE GROUPS

Here's the basic layout of a real estate investment group: a company buys (or builds) apartment or office buildings or retail spaces. Then they offer investors the opportunity to buy individual units, effectively enabling them to join the "group." The company manages all aspects of the property, from securing tenants to setting rents to mowing the lawn. The investors pay a percentage of rent receipts to the company in exchange for those services, and pocket the rest.

Buying Into Building Blocks

Real estate investment groups let investors buy distinct pieces of a larger investment, rather than a portion of the property as a whole; for example, you'd own one specific apartment rather than 10 percent of a ten-apartment building. Typically, your name would be on the lease as the landlord, but the company would take on all of the associated duties.

By participating in more than one group deal, a single investor can hold stakes in multiple large properties. For example, you could buy one apartment in a tower, one office in a building, and one shop in a strip mall, allowing you to diversify into three different types of real estate without having to hold the entire properties.

Vacancy Protection

Most real estate investment group deals offer a form of vacancy protection—something you usually won't have as an individual landlord. Each investor in a property contributes a small percentage of the rent collected from their units into a vacancy pool. Should a unit you own fall vacant, you'd still receive enough cash to cover the mortgage out of the pool until the company secures a new tenant.

RELPS (REAL ESTATE LIMITED PARTNERSHIPS)

RELPs offer a twist on basic real estate investment groups. Not only is the legal structure of the deal different, the investment itself is different in character. Here, you own a percentage of a project rather than a discrete unit.

RELPS are often created by real estate developers looking for financing for large projects (like building a subdivision). The money is used for new construction or significant renovations to existing properties, and the property will not typically produce income until the project is complete.

Limited Partnerships

Limited partnerships (discussed in Chapter 2) are special legal structures created for business purposes. They're made up of at least one general and one limited partner; they can't be the same person, but if there are multiple partners, one person can be both a general and a limited partner. General partners assume all liability for the project and are the only partners that can be directly involved.

Limited partners (also called silent partners) put up money for the deal in exchange for ownership shares.

In RELPs, the general partner is usually a real estate developer (or possibly a property management company) who's trying to raise money for a specific project.

How the Money Works

When you invest in a RELP, you hand over a lump sum of money in exchange for an ownership stake in a real estate project or property. Unlike other types of real estate investing, these don't usually provide regular, steady cash flows (though they can). Instead, you get paid back (hopefully more than you put in) when the property gets sold, which can be years later, and the RELP dissolves.

In some cases, there will be preset intervals where investors can cash out portions of their investment. Even with those intervals, though, RELPs are highly illiquid investments and not suitable if you might need quick access to cash.

INVESTIGATE BEFORE INVESTING

Because real estate investment groups tend to call for large chunks of cash that cannot be returned quickly, it's crucial to perform thorough due diligence before investing. Your investment advisor should take care of the lion's share of this investigation, only presenting you with deals that are suitable for your unique situation. However, you should still carefully evaluate these opportunities before you agree to part with your capital.

Due Diligence

The phrase "due diligence" comes up a lot in relation to real estate investing, especially when you get to investments with higher stakes and less liquidity. Due diligence means conducting an investigation, a sort of background check, before you sign any contracts or hand over any money.

Steps you can take should at least include:

- Carefully reading offering documents and contracts, and having your attorney review them if there's anything (like "legal speak") you don't fully understand.
- Verifying existence of properties held by the real estate investment group or limited partnership (local government maintains ownership records, which are available to the public).
- Checking out the company or general partner as thoroughly as you can through the Better Business Bureau (www.bbb.org), state or local licensing agencies, and their own certified financial statements.
- Asking for proof of other successful properties (vacancy rates, for example) or completed projects, necessary permits and government approvals, and project timelines.

Certified Financial Statements

Companies prepare their own financial statements, which include balance sheets, profit and loss statements, and cash flow statements. Certified financial statements mean that an independent certified public accountant (CPA) has audited and approved those statements. That doesn't mean that every number is perfectly accurate; it means that as a whole, the company's financial picture matches the information in the financial statements.

Beware of Fraud

Because these investments are not regulated the same way as stocks, bonds, and REITs, it's much easier for scam artists to flourish. They aim to especially take advantage of inexperienced real estate investors, so be cautious when entering into these deals.

There are many types of fraudulent real estate investment schemes, and they all rely on enticing novice investors with promises of higher-than-market returns and explosive profits. To avoid getting taken advantage of by unscrupulous parties, look out for these red flags:

- Overblown appraisals
- Skirting the rules for property purchases
- Straw buyers (a proxy buyer used when the real buyer is prohibited from making a transaction)
- Income numbers that don't make any sense

You can find more information and resources to help you avoid fraudulent real estate deals on the Freddie Mac website at www.freddiemac.com.

REAL ESTATE INVESTMENT CLUBS

Join the Club

Investing directly in real estate can be daunting when you're first getting started: buying property is expensive, there's a lot to learn (laws and tax issues, for example), and property maintenance can be overwhelming. Those drawbacks keep a lot of people from participating in real estate investing, despite its many benefits.

How to Find a Club

To find a real estate investing club near you, visit the National Real Estate Investors Association website (https://nationalreia.org). The site has links to local groups throughout the United States. The association also offers a membership with lots of benefits (like discounts at Home Depot) and free educational resources.

Joining an established real estate investment club helps you get up to speed faster, reduces the fear and anxiety that can come from diving into something new without a safety net, and can help you meet your financial goals.

HOW THEY'RE SET UP

Investment clubs (in general) include members who pool their money and make investment decisions as a group. These groups typically have between five and twenty members—big enough to pool enough money to invest in real estate and small enough to be manageable. Because there's a lot of money at stake, real estate investment clubs are normally set up as formal business entities with each member listed as a partial owner.

The Structure

Real estate investment clubs are not informal groups. They're usually set up as LLCs (limited liability companies) or partnerships (see Chapter 2), and each member gets an ownership stake. They have formal by-laws governing the group and the way it invests, including how individual members invest or withdraw money. Normally, they'll elect officers to govern the group.

Most groups require members to commit to a timeframe, agreeing to participate for at least five years (timeframes will vary). A member who decides to leave has to inform the group in writing, as well as find a replacement member that the group approves. Many clubs impose an "early withdrawal" fee on any member who leaves before his or her commitment period is up.

When a property is purchased, the group is listed as the buyer and holds the deed. If a mortgage is required, the group is the legal borrower (though members may have to co-sign the loan).

The Money

When the club is formed, the founding members each contribute a lump sum of money. Whether that contribution is a fixed amount or a minimum depends on how the group is set up. It's easier to track when everyone puts in the same amount, but as long as detailed records are kept and all members agree to it, contributions can vary. Latecomers to the club will also have to contribute a lump sum; this usually happens only when a founding member wants to cash out, so he sells his stake to someone new (who has to be approved by the group). Some clubs also require ongoing contributions (smaller than the original lump sum) to be put toward future investments or club (not property) expenses.

Common REI Philosophy

Before joining a real estate investment club, it's important to know your investing philosophy and theirs. For example, if you're interested in apartment buildings for long-term cash flow, don't join a group that's focused on fixing and flipping distressed properties.

The club will spell out its investment objectives in the by-laws (or other binding agreement). Solidifying that philosophy helps focus the group and develop an investing strategy.

POOLING KNOWLEDGE AND RESOURCES

Real estate investment clubs offer some key advantages over going solo. While money is often the first benefit that springs to mind, it's only one way that working with a group can improve your real estate investing experience.

Access to More Properties

Joining a club gives you options that you wouldn't have as a lone real estate investor just starting out. Clubs can have enough funding to buy multiple properties or even commercial real estate (like office buildings), for example.

Knowledge and Skills

Many real estate investing clubs assign roles to members based on their personal background and abilities. Those responsibilities could include:

- Keeping club records
- Bookkeeping and taxes
- Property maintenance
- Tenant management
- Member communications
- Scheduling meetings
- Representing the club at closings
- Researching potential investments

By keeping these jobs "in-house," the club can direct more funds toward building its real estate portfolio or increasing equity.

Splitting the Difference

When only some members take on club-related jobs, the club can decide to give them additional shares of profits, pay them for their services out of club funds, or decrease their original or ongoing investment amount to compensate them for their work.

Education

Investing smarter is the key to long-term prosperity. Club members meet regularly and share any new experiences or knowledge they've gained (for example, if a member had to deal with an eviction).

Many investment clubs invite expert speakers to address the group on relevant topics, such as local foreclosure laws or how to analyze different real estate markets. Sometimes, club funds are used to send members to real estate–related conferences; the attending members then share what they learned with the whole group.

Networking Connections

Conferences make great networking events. Members can connect with real estate agents, lenders, and other real estate professionals they'd never otherwise come in contact with. Expanding the club's circle of advisors and professionals can offer special access to properties and deals.

AVOID THESE ISSUES

Joining a real estate investment club can have distinct disadvantages, so be careful before you commit your time and money to a club that's not a best fit. Like some other types of real estate investments, a club is illiquid—meaning it's very hard to get your money out if you need it. And unlike other investments, this one is personal in nature; you're a member of a group, which means you're personally connected to the other investors (as they are to each other), and that can cause personal problems down the line.

No Flexibility

The biggest drawback to real estate investment clubs is the complete lack of flexibility for members. If you have a sudden need for your money and have to cash out some of your equity, you'd need to get the support of other members, convince another member to buy out your share, or find a new investor that could take your place in the group to buy you out.

This process can take months, even longer than the process of selling a property. Plus, if you need your money back before the group's stated minimum time commitment is up, you may have to pay a penalty for leaving (and these can be pretty steep). If you can't afford to tie up this money for at least the commitment period, an investment club may not be the right choice for you.

Emotions Run High

Investment clubs are made up of people—and when you combine people and money, emotions are sure to surface. Those feelings can sometimes interfere with sound investment decisions, which can hurt the group's profitability over the long run. For example, some group members can get caught up in the enthusiasm and excitement of a member's property suggestion and overlook property pitfalls. Members may also argue about which properties to buy, hold, or sell.

As with any other group of people, clashes can develop between members, cliques can form, and leaders that drive decisions can emerge. Though members try to keep everything strictly professional, it doesn't always work out that way.

INTERVAL FUNDS
Cash On Schedule

Wealthy and institutional investors have access to investments the rest of us don't, for two key reasons. First, they have more money to invest, so they can access bigger and more profitable assets. Second, they can easily afford to tie up a large portion of their money for years—even decades—without worrying about how or when they'll get it back. Those advantages let them sink money into highly lucrative investments that the rest of us could never touch. That is, we couldn't access these high-level investments until interval funds were born.

Relatively new on the scene (they've only been around since 2014), real estate interval funds are a quickly growing niche. As of this writing, there are still only around a dozen active funds, but expect more to crop up in the near future.

THE INTERVAL ADVANTAGE COMES WITH A CAUTION

Interval funds offer access to otherwise inaccessible investments, ones that normally supply steady income and long-term capital appreciation you won't find with regular funds. But those benefits come with some pretty significant drawbacks, so it's important to understand exactly what you're getting into before you invest in an interval fund.

Special Access

Big-money investors can invest in securities that regular people would never even hear of. These securities are not registered with the SEC. They're not sold on open markets. You have to "know a guy" or have connections to be invited to invest. Plus, most of these deals call for exclusive access, and that means they're closed to all but "accredited investors."

Interval funds help you take part in those exclusive deals no matter who you are. The fund acts as the accredited investor with special access, then turns around and sells pieces to regular investors in affordable chunks.

Accredited Investors

To qualify as an accredited investor, you must have earned at least $200,000 a year ($300,000 for a married couple) for the past two years and reasonably expect that level of income to continue *or* have a net worth of at least $1 million (on your own or joint with your spouse) not including your primary residence.

Liquidity Matters

Interval funds are considered to be semi-liquid. You can't convert your shares into money whenever you want, but you can do that at regular, preset intervals. Typically, the intervals are quarterly, but they may be less frequent (semi-annual or annual). On top of that, you probably won't be able to cash out all of your shares at once; many funds limit the percentage of shares that can be sold during any interval. Bottom line: you sacrifice full liquidity by buying shares of an interval fund but still retain partial liquidity.

The semi-liquid status of interval funds also works as a protection for shareholders. When investors hear bad news about a stock, they panic and a massive sell-off follows, which sends the share price down to dirt cheap levels. That can't happen with interval fund shares because they can't be sold at will.

Liquidity

Liquidity refers to how fast an investment can be converted into cash. A corporate stock, for example, is highly liquid because you can sell it today and have cash in hand tomorrow. A residential rental property, on the other hand, is illiquid because even after you sell it (which can take weeks, months, or longer) you typically still have to wait sixty to ninety days to get your money.

The Long-Term Advantage

When a fund manager doesn't have to constantly worry about having enough cash or liquid assets on hand to meet constant redemptions (as is the case with regular mutual funds), she can take a long-term view. That lets her buy alternative assets like commercial real estate, real estate debt, and shares in high-end private investment funds.

It takes a wealth of experience, dedication, and due diligence to choose the right holdings for the interval fund. That's why so many real estate interval fund managers have been on the job for years, often since the launch. And a well-managed fund will generate substantial, steady returns that far outweigh higher fund fees.

MOVING MONEY IN AND OUT

Like regular mutual funds (called open-end funds), you can buy shares of most interval funds from the issuer (the company that created the fund) whenever you want. Whatever the NAV (net asset value) is on that day is the price you'll pay for each share, plus any sales charges.

Selling your shares is a little more complicated. There are limits on when you can redeem (sell them back to the issuer) your shares, and on how many shares you can redeem at once. That means you can't transform your shares into cash whenever you want, so you have to plan carefully to make sure you don't wind up investment rich but cash poor.

Be Ready for Sticker Shock

Although the buy-ins for real estate interval funds are much smaller than the typical amount invested in such elite holdings, they often run higher than the minimum investment requirements for mutual funds and exchange-traded funds (ETFs). Minimum initial investments typically range from $2,500 to $25,000 (depending on the fund); if you're buying the shares for a retirement account, that minimum may drop to $1,000.

Then come the fees: virtually all interval funds charge a sales fee (or "front-end load") when you buy shares, and those fees typically hover around 5.25 percent. So if you invested $1,000 in a real estate interval fund, you only end up buying $947.50 worth of shares (and paying a sales charge of $52.50). With most funds, you'll also pay a redemption fee (usually around 2 percent) when you sell your shares.

Interval funds also charge more in ongoing fees than managed mutual funds (and substantially more than ultra-low fee index funds). The ongoing expense ratios range from about 2.25 percent to more than 5 percent annually. So for every $1,000 you have invested, you could pay more than $50 in annual fees.

Picking a Real Estate Interval Fund

Real estate interval funds can be hard to track down, and fund information (other than the NAV) can be hard to find. Still, because your money will be locked down, it's important to find out everything you can about the fund before you buy. Once you know the names of funds you might be interested in, go directly to the issuer's website for the most recent documents.

Carefully read the fund prospectus (a legal document that spells out all the fund information in detail) to find accurate information on exactly how to buy and sell shares, initial and ongoing fees, minimum investment requirements, fund management, redemption intervals, and more.

Finding the Funds

You can find a list of real estate interval fund choices on the Interval Fund Tracker website (www.intervalfundtracker.com). Some of the better-known funds in this category include the Griffin Institutional Access Real Estate Fund, the Bluerock Total Income+ Real Estate Fund, and the Vertical Capital Income Fund.

How to Buy and Sell Shares

Most real estate interval funds don't sell shares directly to investors; rather, they sell through registered investment advisors (if you don't have an advisor, the issuer can connect you with one). That's because they want to make sure investors understand that their money will be locked in for a long time, and that's not a good idea for people who don't have either other more liquid investments to rely on or a significant amount of steady income.

INVESTING IN REAL ESTATE DEBT

The IOU Side

There's a saying in the real estate world: "The bank always wins."

That's because when a bank lends money for a property purchase (or anything else, for that matter), it charges interest. When the borrower makes regular payments, the bank wins by collecting interest and profiting. When the borrower doesn't pay, the bank takes the property used as collateral. Either way, the bank wins.

By investing in real estate debt (which comes in a few different forms), you become the bank.

That's not to say there's no risk here. While banks do foreclose on and seize properties, it's not an easy or cheap process. Even with all that, though, the bank never walks away empty-handed.

REAL ESTATE NOTES

Real estate notes (sometimes called mortgage notes) are direct loans to property buyers. While some investors act as private lenders and actually lend the money to borrowers, it's more common for investors to buy existing real estate notes, often at a healthy discount.

When you buy these notes, you will be holding someone's mortgage, as if you were the bank. You collect the payments, you have a lien on the mortgaged property, and you have to deal with the borrower if they stop paying. It sounds like a lot of work, but if you do your homework (called due diligence), all you really have to do is get paid every month.

Look for These Qualities

Real estate notes offer the promise of steady high returns, usually between 5 percent and 9 percent. But like any other investment, not all real estate notes pan out. You can minimize your risk (especially when just starting out) by looking for notes that are:

- **Senior:** first mortgages come first in the pecking order should the borrower default
- **Performing:** notes that are currently and regularly being paid down
- **Seasoned:** older notes that come with a borrower payment track record, so you can see whether someone is actually making regular payments

Due Diligence

Once you've found a pool of senior performing notes, you'll want to drill down to do some more focused due diligence on the specific notes you're considering buying. The four main factors you'll want to investigate are:

1. **Borrower's credit:** Look for whether they're paying their bills regularly and on time, how much debt they have in relation to their income (the debt-to-income ratio, or DTI), and the status of the senior lien.
2. **Borrower's payment history:** The longer someone has been making mortgage payments, the more likely they are to keep doing so; it demonstrates their commitment to the property.
3. **Fair market value (FMV):** Find the current FMV of the property, as it affects the equity (ownership stake) in the property; if the property has declined substantially, you may not be able to recover your investment if the borrower defaults.

4. **Location:** With real estate debt, geography matters for several reasons including state foreclosure laws, local demographics (which can affect future property values), and area economy.

Beware the Risks

The biggest downside risk in note investing comes from borrower delinquencies and defaults. When that happens, you have a few ways to deal with the situation and hopefully avoid foreclosure. Unlike investing in properties, you have several exit strategies available to you with notes. For example, you can help the borrower come up with a payment plan, so neither of you has to deal with foreclosure hassles and the borrower can continue to make regular payments (most people want to stay in their homes). Another option is that you can sell the note to someone else, which you can do much faster than if you were trying to sell a property.

If your borrower does default, make sure you know all the ins and outs of the state law, which covers everything from the foreclosure process to communications to timelines. You may also have to deal with other legal issues, like borrower bankruptcy, property tax liens, or property damage.

MORTGAGE-BACKED SECURITIES (MBS)

Mortgage-backed securities get a bad rap, and a lot of the blame for the 2008 market crash. While they were involved, the problem wasn't the MBS themselves, but rather the millions of bad mortgages used to create them by less scrupulous bankers and investors who didn't really understand what they were buying.

MBS are bonds that use pools of mortgages for collateral. The bond issuer buys up thousands of mortgages, and then repackages them into bonds. As payments are made on the mortgages, the bond issuer passes those payments through to the bondholders (minus their fee, of course). That's why MBS are considered to be "pass-through securities."

Ginnie, Fannie, and Freddie

The three main players in the MBS market are:

- Government National Mortgage Association, or GNMA (pronounced "Ginnie Mae"), is backed by a federal agency and guarantees mortgage payments on loans issued through federal loan programs (like the VA and the FHA). Unlike other MBS, bonds guaranteed by GNMA are backed by the full faith and credit of the US government, just like Treasury bonds.
- Federal National Mortgage Association, or FNMA ("Fannie Mae"), is a private corporation that buys mortgages from large commercial banks, repackages them into bonds, and sells those bonds to investors. FNMA is not backed by the federal government (even though the government created it), so these bonds carry higher credit risk (the risk that you won't get your money back).
- Federal Home Loan Mortgage Corporation, or FHLMC (commonly called "Freddie Mac"), works almost the same way as FNMA. It buys up mortgages from smaller lenders, like savings and loan banks or credit unions, then packages them to create MBS. Freddie Mac bonds are not backed by the US government.

Benefits for Investors

MBS offer a variety of benefits to investors who want to profit from the real estate markets without actually holding property.

- **Monthly cash:** Unlike other bonds, MBS send monthly payments to investors, but the principal and interest amounts vary every month. That's because payments are dependent on the underlying mortgages, and the principal and interest portion of payments shift every month as the loan balances decrease.
- **Strong credit quality:** GNMA, FNMA, or FHLMC securities come with high credit scores, especially compared with private-label MBS or other corporate bonds. That means the chance you won't get your money back is very slim.
- **High yields:** MBS usually pay higher interest rates than Treasury bonds and even some corporate bonds. That's partly due to their unpredictable cash flows and that they're often harder to sell than Treasury bonds.

MBS also offer another advantage to real estate investors: geographic diversification. Because the underlying mortgages come from all over the country, localized housing market blips can be offset by the rest of the pool.

The Risks

MBS face all of the regular risks (changing interest rates, for example) linked to bonds and other fixed-income securities, and two that are unique to them. These special risks are tied to the underlying mortgages: homeowners could default (stop making payments, substantially more likely with private-label MBS) or pay off their loans early, either of which would affect investor yield and cash flows.

Mortgage Debt on the Rise

As of September 30, 2018, Americans owe more than $9 trillion in mortgage debt. That's up almost $400 billion from 2017, and up more than $140 billion from June of 2018. Yet even with all that debt, mortgage delinquency rates remain at 1.2 percent, about four times lower than credit card delinquencies.

In a period of rising interest rates, prepayment risk decreases; people typically refinance when interest rates drop. When interest rates fall and homeowners do prepay, investors receive interest payments for a shorter time period than expected. Default risk is much lower now since banks have increased lending standards.

How to Invest in MBS

MBS can be harder to buy and sell than other types of bonds, as they're bought mainly by institutional investors. Many MBS are issued and sold in large denominations (like $25,000 minimums), but some are issued at $1,000 (like most other types of bonds). You can trade MBS through specialty bond brokers, which you can find at most major brokerages (like Charles Schwab or Merrill Edge).

The easiest way to invest in MBS is through specialty mutual funds or ETFs. Though technically MBS are not fixed-income investments (because the payments can vary monthly), they're usually included in that category (because they're bonds).

CHAPTER 5

NEW TRENDS IN REI

Though real estate is the oldest investment in the world, the investment options are continually evolving, offering new and exciting trends to real estate investors. As innovations like blockchain add liquidity to real estate investing and crowdfunding lowers the entry bar for this lucrative asset class, more people than ever are able to take advantage of the many benefits of this wealth-building strategy.

Investors can tap into cutting-edge trends from eco-housing to senior cohousing, take advantage of the enormous tax benefits to be found in Opportunity Zones, and have more access than ever before to properties all over the world. The potential for profit is virtually unlimited, as real estate investing continues to change with the times.

CROWDFUNDED REAL ESTATE

Mob Money

Crowdfunding helps level the playing field for real estate investors, letting you put up (relatively) small amounts of cash to participate in high-end real estate deals. It's a newer twist on the growing crowd-funding industry, which covers everything from helping people cover enormous medical bills (like through a GoFundMe page) to raising money to launch a company (like on Indiegogo). Through crowdfunding, individual investors can get in on otherwise inaccessible investments such as office complexes or high-rise apartment buildings.

Crowdfunded sites typically offer real estate investment opportunities in either equity (ownership) or debt, but some include a mix of the two. Before investing in any crowdfunded real estate deals, make sure to read the prospectus (or other offering document) and fully understand exactly what you're investing in.

WHAT'S CROWDFUNDING?

Crowdfunding is a new way to raise money, using social media (like Twitter and Facebook) to spread the word about new investment opportunities. Entrepreneurs looking for start-up funding have been turning to this new business model in record numbers. Now the idea has been expanded to allow more access to real estate investments.

While the goals are a little different, the process is the same. Originally geared toward accredited investors (high net worth individuals), the platform has opened up to anyone who can scare up a site's minimum investment, which usually ranges from $500 to $25,000. That's because this is an illiquid market; you can't just sell your investment on a secondary market (like the stock exchange) when you need your money back.

Because these investments happen online only, investors face an increased risk for fraud and security breaches. You can limit your risk exposure by thoroughly investigating the platform and its security features (though virtually no site is 100 percent hack-proof).

How It Works

Crowdfunding works by pooling small amounts of money from a lot of investors to finance one or more property investments. In return, each investor owns a proportional piece of the project, a passive, indirect real estate investment. These are long-term investments, with a minimum time requirement that investors must commit to, so be prepared for your money to be locked up for a while. Like most types of investment funds, most platforms charge fees that normally run somewhere in the 0.5 percent to 2 percent range, but can vary depending on the specific platform.

These investments may promise high returns (10 percent to 25 percent, for example) but come with a lot of risk. Projects can fall through, cash flow projections can fall short, and investors can be left with nothing when things go wrong. When everything goes right though, you could walk away with much higher returns than you'd earn on more traditional investments.

The Platforms

There are hundreds of crowdfunded investment platforms for real estate—but they aren't all the same. They all have different niches (such as the type of properties they invest in) and different strategies. In addition to knowing the deal details, make sure you do your due diligence on the platform you're using. You'll want to consider factors like platform reputation and track record, fees, minimum investments, investor protections (in case a deal falls through), and investment options.

Reputable crowdfunded real estate investment platforms include:

- Fundrise (www.fundrise.com)
- Patch of Land (www.patchofland.com)
- RealtyMogul (www.realtymogul.com)
- Groundfloor (www.groundfloor.us)
- PeerStreet (www.peerstreet.com)

Each has different offerings and different strengths. Make sure the platform you choose fits with your investment goals and style.

A Word About RealtyShares

Investors were dumbstruck when crowdfunding pioneer RealtyShares closed its doors to new investors after experiencing serious financial trouble. It's not surprising that one company would falter in a relatively new industry. It doesn't signal that crowdfunded investing is a bad idea, just that you need to carefully screen any platform before handing over your money.

EQUITY OR DEBT?

There are two main ways to take part in crowdfunded real estate investing: equity and debt. While the vast majority of platforms are in equity investing, there are plenty of options for investing in real estate debt. Both types require time commitments, with the equity periods usually longer than the debt periods.

Pick a Property

One of the most attractive features of crowdfunded real estate investing is choice. In many platforms, investors can focus on specific properties or projects, something not available with other types of indirect real estate investments (like REITs). You can also direct money to a few different individual properties, creating your own mini real estate fund.

When you invest in equity, you own a piece of a property, which may be under development or renovation; when you invest in debt, you're lending money to finance a property. In the pecking order, if a project goes south, debt investors have priority over equity investors.

Equity Side

With an equity crowdfunded platform, each investor owns a piece of a property (or portfolio of properties) purchased by the fund. Income comes typically from rents, passed through to investors as dividends, and gains when a property is sold for a profit.

Equity investments are normally locked in for a period of three to ten years. When the preset period is up, investors get their money back (unless something goes wrong with the project, which does happen). When things go as planned, investors will receive periodic (usually quarterly) dividends, with the outstanding balance paid out at the end, possibly with a big gain (due to appreciation).

Because so much can go wrong with these investments, they are considered high risk. But the unlimited upside potential for returns still attracts savvy investors willing to place that bet.

Debt Side

On the debt side of crowdfunded real estate investing, earnings come from mortgage loan payments. The platform holds a mortgage loan on a specific property (or group of properties), and passes the interest along to investors as payments are collected.

In this space, debt investments are less risky than equity investments for a few reasons:

- Shorter lock-in period, usually two years or less, which doesn't tie up your money as long
- Secured mortgage debt, so if the borrower doesn't pay, the platform can foreclose on the property and sell it, returning at least some money to investors
- Predictable income, based on the stated interest rate of the mortgage loan(s)

These investments typically have returns in the 8 percent to 12 percent range (never higher than the rate on the underlying loan), which may be paid out monthly or quarterly. Fees on crowdfunded debt are usually higher than on the equity side and may involve additional loan origination fees.

SENIOR COHOUSING BOOM

Turning Silver Into Gold

As a huge population of baby boomers heads toward retirement, more and more of them are turning toward communal living and cohousing communities that cater toward older adults. An increasing number of seniors don't want to live alone and don't need the round-the-clock care offered by assisted living communities. The cohousing model serves multiple purposes for seniors (mainly financial and social) and comes in different forms, from condos to private homes to apartment communities with shared social spaces.

The demand for this type of housing is growing rapidly, as even the youngest baby boomers are edging toward retirement, making it a perfect opportunity for investors to get in on the ground floor. Right now, there are only twenty-two completed senior housing communities in the US, with more in the planning and construction phases (according to the Cohousing Association of the United States). That leaves a lot of room for growth in this constantly expanding market—which could mean a lot of profit potential for real estate investors.

Keep in mind that these aren't like regular neighborhoods; they're intentional communities where people are expected to participate and contribute to the group in some way. The people living there have common values and intentions, like living healthy lifestyles in environmentally friendly spaces, embracing lifelong learning, and dedication to community.

THE BABY BOOMER GENERATION

Technically, most of the baby boomers aren't seniors yet—and even the ones closest don't think of themselves that way. This generation covers the 75.4 million people born between 1946 and 1964, where the oldest are just in their early seventies; although some people would call them senior citizens, many of these elders consider age eighty to be the cutoff for that category. To that end, they aren't ready for what most people think of as "senior living"—assisted living facilities and nursing homes.

Because people are living longer and staying healthier, remaining active in their later years, the old concepts of senior housing have been overturned, making way for reimagined designs and functionality. These new-style models focus more on community and activity, perfect for the growing movement toward senior cohousing.

Follow the Demographics

One of the biggest trends among baby boomers is the desire to live among like-minded people in their age range. They favor organized activities and easy access to services from gyms to dry cleaners. Plus, this generation of soon-to-be seniors is much more tech-savvy then the prior generation. Comfortable with smart technology, they expect their living spaces to be packed with the latest voice-activated amenities.

Another trend is the shift from owning to renting. According to an analysis by RentCafé, the number of renters aged fifty-five and older increased by 28 percent (about 2.5 million people) between 2009 and 2015 (the latest census data available). That coincided with a 21 percent jump in rentals by families with no minor children in the home. Basically, older empty-nesters are increasingly moving away from homeownership and toward the flexibility of rentals.

Forward-thinking developers are jumping on these trends, creating active-living communities that fill these requirements. Some are creating roommate-style dwellings (similar to college dorm suites) where a pair (or a few) residential units share some common space. Others combine private homes in a sort of clustered community arrangement, with a central space that acts as a common house featuring a kitchen and dining area, a social area (like a den), and laundry facilities.

Increased Longevity and "Healthspan"

Over the past few decades, lifespans and "healthspans" (which basically refers to how long people live in good health) have gotten longer, and the continuing trends in healthy living predict those spans are going to keep increasing. That's led to much greater demand for activity centers—and not just the stereotypical golf courses. This demographic is demanding homes that are within walking distance of amenities like cultural attractions and shopping. They're all about active living, and shy away from spaces that center around medical care or assisted living.

The Healthcare Piece

In communities where the minimum age hovers around sixty, there will be tenants who become ill or disabled. That's why it's important, before you invest, to make sure the management group running the community has experience dealing with seniors.

COHOUSING INVESTMENT
OPPORTUNITIES

There are two main ways to invest in senior cohousing: directly and indirectly. Most individual investors take the indirect route, as there's more opportunity for diversity with smaller cash outlays. But there's also great opportunity for steady and reliable rental income streams for landlords who snap up properties in up-and-coming housing communities.

Strong Returns

Over the past ten years, investments in senior housing have outpaced other types of real estate investments, including industrial, retail, and hotels (according to the National Council of Real Estate Investment Fiduciaries [NCREIF]). While this does include assisted living and memory-driven facilities, it still speaks to an overall trend toward profits in the senior sector.

Either way, with ten thousand Americans turning sixty-five every day, there's bound to be huge demand over both the short and long terms for this type of housing. Investors who put their money in the right places now can lock in income for years to come.

Buy Properties

One way to cash in on the coming silver boom: buy properties in senior cohousing communities and rent them out. Seniors tend to make more reliable, stable tenants as they're often reluctant to move once they've found a safe, comfortable, affordable place. Plus, many value the cohousing lifestyle over that of standard retirement communities.

Communities that offer communal amenities can help you score even more lucrative rentals. Some common amenities include:

- On-site dry-cleaning services
- Recreation and fitness centers
- Workspaces
- On-site transportation
- Social activities

Be aware that many cohousing communities screen residents to make sure they'll fit in with the other people living there, which may make it a little harder to find tenants. On the other hand, some cohousing communities have waiting lists, building in a prospective tenant pool.

Invest In Builders

Another way to take advantage of the impending senior cohousing boom is by investing in the companies that will build the communities, and even the companies that will supply their building materials.

Other Ways to Invest

If you want to invest in senior cohousing without such a big commitment, you have other choices. For one thing, you can look at REITs (real estate investment trusts) in this sector. Senior living REITs offer all the benefits of property ownership (steady income, asset appreciation) without the full risk profile. Plus, REITs typically hold a broad portfolio of commercial properties, giving you an instantly diversified investment. Make sure that the REIT specializes in the type of senior cohousing you want to invest in, rather than in properties like nursing homes. You can find a full listing of holdings in the REIT's prospectus.

You can also invest in senior housing through a crowdfunded platform called Senior Living Fund. The platform has been around since 2015 and is currently funding its third and fourth projects. Right now, this platform is open to only accredited investors, and the lowest minimum investment is $50,000.

This investment space—specifically senior cohousing—is relatively new, but as the sector grows, expect to see more REITs, funds, and crowdfunding platforms start to appear.

OPPORTUNITY ZONES GET MORE ATTRACTIVE

The Wonderful World of OZ

In 2017, the US Congress created a new community development program to promote long-term investment in low-income or financially distressed areas—called Opportunity Zones—throughout the country. To invest in these OZ and reap special tax benefits, investments have to be made through Qualified Opportunity Funds, which have to invest at least 90 percent of their capital in OZ. The stated point of the funds is to bring development and redevelopment into underserved areas that desperately need improvement.

The rules surrounding these investments can be a little confusing, but as they get tested in 2019 (on 2018 tax returns), a lot of questions and uncertainties will be clarified.

Keep in mind that investing in OZ is a long-term prospect, so investors who may need to cash out before the ten-year mark should look at other alternatives.

OPPORTUNITY FUNDS

The only way to invest in OZ and reap substantial tax benefits is through Qualified Opportunity Funds (QOFs). These funds are geared to wealthy investors with long investment time horizons (at least ten years). Because one of the key benefits involves deferring capital gains tax, these funds are perfect for investors who've just earned sizeable gains through asset sales. By putting those gains into a QOF, the capital gains tax can be avoided until the fund investment is sold or December 31, 2026 (whichever comes first).

The IRS defines a Qualified Opportunity Fund as a partnership or corporation that is "organized for the purpose of investing in qualified opportunity zone property." What that really means is this: the company certifies itself as a QOF with IRS Form 8996, with an official starting date for investment (nothing invested before that qualifies). Then the QOF collects money from investors and uses at least 90 percent of that money to invest in "qualified opportunity zone property."

Qualified Opportunity Zone Property

Once an Opportunity Fund is formed, it has to start putting money into an OZ, and there are three ways it can invest there and maintain QOF status:

1. New tangible property (like construction equipment)
2. New or substantially renovated real estate (renovations have to cost more than the purchase price of the property)
3. An operating business

There are some kinds of businesses that those investment funds can't be used for, such as country clubs, racetracks, and casinos.

Designated OZ

Opportunity Zones are census tracts (special areas) designated by state governors and federal agencies as targets for economic development. The areas were selected based on income and poverty levels, but in some cases that didn't provide a true picture of the area's needs. For example, college towns appear to be low-income areas because they're populated mainly by students, even though those areas in general may not be distressed.

Examples of designated OZ include areas in:

- Oakland, California
- Los Angeles, California
- Seattle, Washington
- Phoenix, Arizona

Where's the Opportunity?

More than 8,700 Opportunity Zones, approximately 12 percent of all census tracts, have been certified by the US Treasury. At least 19 percent of those (according to the Brookings Institution) are in already gentrifying areas (meaning development is ongoing), and many OZ are very close to or based in areas ripe for growth, a winning formula for investors. You can find a complete list of OZ at www.cdfifund.gov.

FINDING OPPORTUNITY

So far, OZ investment is geared to accredited investors and very high net worth individuals, with minimum investments starting at $25,000. That could change over the next couple of years, as interest and activity increase. For now, these funds work best for people who've just scored a large taxable capital gain and want to defer the tax hit (for example, you sold an investment property for a $250,000 profit and don't want to buy another one, but also don't want to face a current 20 percent tax bite).

Invest In Opportunity Funds

If you have plenty of cash on hand to invest—especially if that cash is tied to a capital gain—you can get in on one of the dozens of already existing Opportunity Funds. In the near future, we're sure to see many more Opportunity Funds crop up, and those are likely to be in the more needy areas (as there's already a lot of investment in the already gentrifying zones).

Some of the more well-known currently operating Opportunity Funds include:

- Fundrise Opportunity Fund
- The Pearl Fund
- Access Ventures Opportunity Fund
- Emergent Communities Fund

You can find a full listing of Opportunity Funds (along with other valuable information) at www.ncsha.org, the National Council of State Housing Agencies's website.

Opportunities to Come

You don't have to be a person to invest in an Opportunity Fund. That means corporations, LLCs, partnerships, and REITs can invest. In turn, that will lead to more opportunities for regular investors who don't have huge minimum investments to fork over.

GOING INTERNATIONAL

The Global Ground Game

Some of the most lucrative real estate investment opportunities lie outside the United States. The US has a mature real estate industry, and that means slower growth than in places where the sector is just starting to find footing. That growth potential can be found all over the world, adding another layer of diversification to US-heavy portfolios.

Developing Returns

According to Nareit, real estate in emerging markets has been outpacing that in developed countries at an astounding pace. Over a three-year period from 2014–2017, overall emerging market real estate investments returned 7.80 percent compared to 4.63 percent in developed nations. Over a single year (September 2016–September 2017), the difference is even greater: 28.40 percent for emerging versus a measly 0.84 percent for developed.

The foreign real estate market includes countries with a newly created or growing middle class and expanding economies, developing countries with dirt cheap (for now) real estate, and countries popular with tourists (looking for vacation rentals) and ex-pats (looking for permanent homes). Just as with US real estate, there are direct and indirect investment opportunities overseas, both of which may increase your portfolio's stability and profitability.

BENEFITS AND DRAWBACKS

Investing in foreign real estate has a lot of earnings potential along with some increased risks. But when they make up just a portion of your total holdings, international investments can bring balance and enhanced returns. Because they're not tied to the US real estate or stock markets, global real estate investments won't follow the same ups and downs.

The Advantages of Going Global

Putting some money into real estate investments outside the United States offers unique benefits, whether you buy physical properties or indirect securities (like real estate investment trusts or exchange-traded funds). Investing internationally helps blunt portfolio losses specific to the United States, such as a dip in the economy or housing market. It also gives you access to developing economies that are poised for explosive growth (barring natural disasters or political instability). Countries in growth mode need more housing, more infrastructure, and more commercial development to support an influx of opportunities; as millions of people join the "middle class," real estate flourishes.

On the Personal Side

Buying an investment property in a country you want to visit extensively or live in gives you a double helping of benefits. Through rent and property appreciation, your global getaway pays for itself and provides pre-relocating cash flow. Then, when you're ready to be there, you already have a substantial holding and history in the country.

Know the Drawbacks

Global investing comes with its own extra set of risks, beyond typical investment or real estate risks, such as:

- Political risk, particularly regarding land rights
- Taxation risk, because investing outside the US can negate some regular real estate tax benefits
- Currency risk, since asset values and distributions are tied to exchange rates
- Liquidity risk, as overseas investments can be harder to sell (especially physical properties)

In addition, you may be faced with higher (sometimes substantially higher) transaction costs and tougher restrictions when buying or selling foreign real estate investments.

AROUND THE WORLD WITH REITS AND FUNDS

Indirect international real estate investing can help shield you from some of the bigger downside risks (like currency risk) while still letting you participate in the global real estate renaissance. Though for a long time only the US and Australia had REITs on the market, now thirty-seven countries (including France, Hong Kong, and Kenya) allow REITs, with eleven additional countries considering enacting REIT legislation. Plus, the field has greatly expanded, with nearly five hundred real estate companies (REITs and other types of companies allowed overseas) to choose from holding around $1.5 trillion in assets. You can buy shares of individual REITs (usually on foreign exchanges) or invest in an ETF that holds multiple international REITs. Since global REITs can be tough to track down, it's easier for beginning investors to start with REIT ETFs. Expect these funds to have higher fees than strictly US-based funds.

Solid global real estate ETFs include:

- Vanguard Global ex-US Real Estate ETF (VNQI)
- WisdomTree Global ex-US Real Estate Fund (DRW)
- iShares International Developed Real Estate ETF (IFGL)

Before you dive in, here's an important point to keep in mind: emerging market real estate investment offers the potential for higher returns, but also comes with a lot of risk and volatility (values bounce around). That means your investments can also bring substantially lower—even negative—returns as well.

BUYING FOREIGN PROPERTIES

Buying land overseas comes with a lot of unfamiliar factors, from stamp duties (a sort of document tax) to sales restrictions. Before you commit to buying a property outside the US, make sure you are completely familiar with the country's property, foreign ownership, and landlord laws; doing some thorough research will save you tons of headaches going forward.

For example, many countries don't have the same idea of property rights as the US, so even if you buy a property you may not own it outright. Other countries don't allow foreign nationals to own property at all, but that may not stop someone from selling it to you.

What all this really means is that you must make sure you know all the rules before you buy investment real estate in another country.

Cash Matters

It's nearly impossible and very expensive to get a mortgage in another country. For one thing, not every country has mortgage lending. When they do, it's not the same as taking out a loan in the US. Depending on the norms in the particular country, down payment requirements (for foreign nationals, which you would be) can be as large as 50 percent of the property value, and interest rates can be very high. On top of that, local banks may demand that you take out a life insurance policy with the bank as the beneficiary. On the flip side, US banks virtually never lend money for overseas property.

Check the Listings

You can find foreign property listings and local guidelines on dedicated websites like Global Property Guide (www.globalpropertyguide.com) and Everything Overseas (www.everythingoverseas.com). Realtor.com (www.realtor.com) also has an international property listings section.

That leaves cash as the main option for buying real estate abroad. The deal will go much more smoothly and quickly and probably cost less; you're more likely to get a better price when you bring cash to the table. Beware: make sure to only pay cash for real estate that is already built rather than in development. Yes, developers may offer financing, but a lot can go wrong, and it will be very hard to recover (if not impossible) your investment if the project plans fall through.

Know the Rules

The most important thing you need to know before buying investment property outside the US is the country's take on 100 percent deeded freehold property. That means the property you buy is completely and only yours. When a country doesn't recognize this, it means that the government can *at any time* come and claim the property. Some countries that do offer deeded freehold property in general still bar foreign nationals from 100 percent outright ownership. Before you invest, find out how property ownership for foreigners works in that country.

Other global guidelines are quirkier. For example, in some countries, foreigners are allowed to own real estate but not land, meaning you could buy condos but not freestanding houses. In other places, foreigners are allowed to sell property but not take the sale proceeds out of the country. Many countries strictly limit where and how much property foreigners can buy. On top of all that, you'll also need to know the country's visa requirements before you embark on your property purchase. To make sure you've got all the legalities covered, find a local real estate lawyer to handle your deal.

Use an International Broker

To simplify your foreign property purchase, work with an experienced international broker, a real estate company with offices around the world. Two of the most prominent international real estate firms include Sotheby's International Realty and Christie's International Real Estate.

ECO-HOUSING

Go Green to Grow Your Green

Going green isn't just good for the planet—it can boost the returns on your real estate investments, sometimes substantially. Eco-housing is a movement where homes are built or renovated to minimize their carbon footprint and impact on the environment. It encompasses things like sustainable building materials, energy-efficient design, and water-conserving appliances.

While this new direction does focus largely on homes, it also covers other types of real estate such as office buildings, retail centers, and medical facilities—places where people work, shop, and heal. From an investment perspective, this is a growing and potentially highly profitable trend, geared toward long-term returns. Not only does going green reduce property-carrying costs, it also increases revenue streams; all that while helping the environment is a triple win for investors.

HOW TO GREENHAB

"Greenhabbing," the practice of renovating properties with an environmentally friendly slant, is one of the hottest trends in real estate. Whether your plan is to fix-and-flip or hold-and-rent, you can increase property profitability by going green. Though this process may seem expensive and overwhelming at first, the costs will be greatly outweighed by all the benefits you'll reap.

Even small improvements can have a big impact on both the environment and your investment bottom line. Examples of eco-friendly improvements include:

- Energy-efficient appliances
- Low-flow toilets and showerheads
- Solar panels
- Green building materials and supplies

Financial Assistance for Going Green

To jump-start green initiatives, the US government and several nonprofit organizations offer financial incentives to property owners. These programs may offer tax credits, rebates, and grants for greenhabbing projects. Visit the US Department of Energy (www.energy.gov/savings) to learn more.

Get Your Property Eco-Certified

If you decide to greenhab your properties, take the extra step to have them certified by every appropriate program. Doing that proves to prospective tenants or buyers that the home meets the qualifying standards and regulations, and that you're not just jumping on the "going green" bandwagon.

The most common certifications include:

- LEED (Leadership in Energy and Environmental Design), an internationally recognized green building rating and certification system
- HERS (Home Energy Rating System), a nationally recognized rater of a building's energy efficiency
- Energy Star, a US government-backed symbol for energy-efficient products

HIGHER INVESTMENT
RETURNS AND ADDED VALUE

Making green changes to buildings saves energy, reduces green-house gas emissions, and decreases water consumption, and it also makes a very positive difference to the financial bottom line for real estate investments, whether they're direct or indirect.

With direct real estate investment, adding green features to your investment properties boosts their value and profitability (even more than standard improvements) in several key ways:

- **Reduced energy bills.** LEED-certified homes can save as much as 20 percent on energy costs, and solar panels can greatly lower monthly energy bills.
- **Increased equity.** Certified green property improvements immediately increase the appraisal (by as much as 10 percent) and market value, giving real estate investors an instant equity bump.
- **Higher rent levels.** Tenants are willing to pay more to live in certified green buildings, according to the National Multifamily Housing Council.
- **Higher resale value.** Homebuyers are willing to pay $15,000 more for a home with solar panels, according to a study from UC Berkeley—and that's just one possible green improvement.

Eco-friendly renovations also bring quality-of-life improvements to tenants or future buyers. For example, building with green, sustainable materials can reduce toxin, indoor pollutant, and allergen levels.

On top of that, greenhabbing will help attract more renters (for landlords and REITs) and homebuyers (for house flippers). Millennials make up 32 percent of the home-buying population, and they want their homes to be sustainable, efficient, and smart. By 2020, members of Gen Z will make up 40 percent of the population; this group is focused on the environment and interested in eco-friendly housing.

Rising Interest

According to a survey by Cushman & Wakefield (an American real estate services firm), real estate investors and tenants (both residential and commercial) are calling for more sustainable building practices. That demand has turned green initiatives into a competitive advantage that benefits investors.

That interest benefits indirect real estate investors as well: as investors demand more socially responsible investing, REITs have substantially increased their sustainable building holdings. To get in on the green real estate trend without holding properties, look at REITs like:

- Camden Property Trust (CPT)
- Prologis (PLD)
- Digital Realty Trust (DLR)
- Macerich (MAC)

BLOCKCHAIN TECHNOLOGY
Building Blocks

Articles and discussions about blockchain are all over the web, touching millions of people and businesses, even though it's still mysterious and confusing for the vast majority. At its core, blockchain is just a new tech-based way of doing things we already do, but with an added layer of accountability and security.

The real estate industry is just beginning to dip its toe in the blockchain ocean, and this new technology will revolutionize the way we buy and sell property and investments. By adding efficiency and speed, reducing costs, and enhancing security, blockchain is poised to make real estate investing even easier and more accessible for regular investors.

BLOCKCHAIN BASICS

Blockchain is a virtual decentralized transaction-recording program. Here's what that means: it exists only online, making it virtual. There's no single central database (that could be hacked) but rather a series of thousands (maybe millions) of individual computers that all record the same transaction. The program is like a giant ledger that keeps track of every piece of every transaction. Because every record is encrypted, and every computer in the series sees the same record, the ledger is essentially hack-proof.

That's hugely different from the banks, credit card companies, and other information holders that keep records now. With all of the data breaches of the past few years, it's obvious that those older systems aren't as secure as we all hoped they were. Blockchain technology changes that.

Blockchain Is *Not* Bitcoin

Blockchain and cryptocurrencies are tied together, but they are not the same thing. Cryptocurrencies are virtual currencies that rely on blockchain technology. Blockchain lets people and businesses transfer money without having to go through a third party like Venmo, PayPal, or a bank. Blockchain is simply the framework that lets that transfer happen in a secure, traceable way.

The Block and the Chain

Blockchain works like digital data storage, where each piece of information is held in a tamper-proof block. Each block gets assigned a unique identifier called a *hash*, and it's based on the information contained in the block. Any change to the block—even something tiny like adding a period or deleting a single letter—automatically changes the block's hash.

The hash is also how blocks get chained together. For example, if Block 2 refers to Block 1's hash, the two blocks get chained (the blockchain). A change to Block 1, which results in a changed hash, automatically unchains Blocks 1 and 2. On a larger scale, any change to a single block means every other block in the chain would have to be changed to keep them connected. That's what makes blockchain so secure: you can't just change one block, making the information contained in each block tamper-proof.

Removing Middlemen

When people want to move money, they have to go through some sort of intermediary (like a bank) to facilitate a wire transfer or an ACH (account clearing house) transaction. That takes days (sometimes longer) and often imposes a fee on at least one of the parties to the transaction.

Blockchain gets rid of the need for middlemen. People can transfer money (and other information) directly using blockchain, saving both time and money.

TRANSFORMING REAL ESTATE INVESTING

Blockchain has the potential to forever change the way we buy, sell, and invest in real estate. It will vastly simplify and speed up the property transaction process, giving investors more flexibility. The blockchain process is more transparent, accurate, and secure than the traditional real estate transaction, reducing costs and risk for investors.

Blockchain is expected to disrupt the real estate industry in key ways:

- **Verify property details:** exact location, floor plans, renovations, safety reports, and green certifications will all be part of a property's hash.
- **Quick loan decisions:** borrower information stored digitally can be transmitted securely and completely in seconds.
- **Information limits:** block viewers will only be able to see the portion of information that's relevant.

These changes are just the beginning of how blockchain can transform real estate transactions.

Property Tokens

Through blockchain, investors gain the capability to invest in property tokens, which represent a direct ownership stake in a particular piece of real estate. A company, such as a REIT, buys a commercial property and divides it up into a fixed number of pieces using blockchain technology. When investors buy in, they get tokens that act like regular securities (such as stocks or REIT shares), entitled to dividend payments and able to be sold on a secondary market.

Liquid Real Estate

One common complaint among real estate investors is the lack of liquidity, especially with direct or unlisted property investments. Blockchain tokens bring liquidity to real estate investments, because they can be more easily traded on secondary markets, rather than having to wait for a building to be sold to cash out.

The first such offering happened in 2018 with a student housing building called The Hub in South Carolina. Each token is especially coded to follow property ownership and investment laws to make sure that none are sold to anyone disallowed (by law). This is the first tokenized REIT made available to investors, and others are expected to follow soon.

Simplified Title

Real estate investors need to make sure that they have clear title, free of liens and other ownership claims, and that can be an exhausting exercise. Every local government has its own way of managing property records: some use online databases, others still rely on hard-copy paper trails. Both can be riddled with errors and missing data, which is why title insurance is a $15 billion industry.

While it will take a lot of time, money, and effort to get started, moving this information onto the blockchain would substantially increase the efficiency and accuracy of the title search process. Plus, as changes were made to lots and buildings, it could be added to the blockchain so information about the property would be up-to-date and correct (a *Forbes* article referred to it as "Carfax for homes"). We're not there yet, but expect to see this happen within the next few years.

CHAPTER 6

PAY LESS TAXES AND KEEP MORE OF YOUR MONEY

Like all other kinds of income, taxes eat into investment profits. While you probably can't avoid them completely, there are a lot of things you can do to keep the tax bite as small as possible. In fact, in some cases, real estate investments may produce tax losses even when you're collecting cash—it's one of their greatest potential benefits. Take time to learn the ins and outs of real estate tax rules, or find a tax preparer who's experienced in this area. There are lots of loopholes to take advantage of...if you know exactly where to look.

SPECIAL REAL ESTATE TAX RULES

Building Tax Shelters

On top of all the income and cash flow real estate investments can generate, they also come with special tax benefits that can save you a lot of money. The Tax Cuts and Jobs Act of 2017 was kind to real estate investors and especially advantageous to landlords. The new law protects some old advantages unique to real estate investment and adds a wealth of new benefits.

That said, the new tax law isn't yet *fully* understood; it's important to enlist professional tax help to make sure you take advantage of every possible deduction. It could take years for the IRS to figure out how they'll interpret some of the new rules, so make sure your tax preparer is aware of the most current rulings.

SPECIAL DEDUCTIONS AND BENEFITS

Real estate investing comes with several tax benefits that simply aren't available for other types of investments. Depreciation—an on-paper expense that reduces taxable income and ends up providing positive cash flow—is the one most people know about, but there are more. For example, a unique "trading up" provision called 1031 exchanges lets you sell and buy property without paying capital gains taxes on profits (more on that later in this chapter). Another bonus: passive earnings (like real estate investing) aren't subject to Social Security and Medicare taxes, another huge savings.

Special Rules for REIT Dividends

REIT investors will get extra benefits from the new tax laws (the Tax Cuts and Jobs Act, or TCJA), making REITs an even better investment option. Unlike "qualified" stock dividends that get taxed at special more-favorable rates, the dividends from REITs get sliced and diced into three categories that determine their tax treatment. The categories work like this:

- Ordinary income, which is taxed at your regular income tax rate
- Capital gains distributions, which get taxed at favorable long-term capital gains tax rates that top out at 20 percent
- Return of capital, which isn't taxable now, but could increase your capital gains tax bill when you sell the investment

This sounds complicated, but it will all be laid out on the single Form 1099-DIV you receive from the REIT. And if you're holding REITs in your retirement account (especially a highly tax-beneficial Roth IRA), you won't have to worry about it at all.

Long-Term Capital Gains

Other than house flipping, real estate investments are normally held long term. When they're eventually sold, they qualify for long-term capital gains rates, which are much lower than ordinary income tax rates.

What's a Capital Gain?

Capital assets are property that is owned for longer than one year and not sold in the normal course of business (like inventory in a shop). When you sell a capital asset for more than you paid for it (i.e., you make a profit), you have a capital gain.

Any property that you hold for longer than one year before selling it gets the long-term capital gains treatment. Depending on your personal filing status and income, your rate will be either 0 percent, 15 percent, or 20 percent. For example, if you file as single, and your taxable income is below $38,600, you would pay no taxes, 0 percent, on any long-term capital gains.

BONUS DEPRECIATION FOR LANDLORDS

There's a special tax provision called Section 179 that lets business owners deduct 100 percent of the cost of personal property (such as desks and computers) in the year it was bought instead of having to depreciate it over time. In the past, rental property owners weren't allowed to use this provision for personal property (such as appliances, carpets, and furniture) in their rental units. The Tax Cuts and Jobs Act (TCJA) removed that restriction, and now landlords can take full advantage of Section 179 deductions, up to a total of $1 million (but the deduction can't *create* a net loss).

The TCJA also offers an added "bonus depreciation." Before TCJA, business owners were limited to bonus depreciation of up to 50 percent of the cost of a *new* asset in the year it was purchased. Now bonus depreciation has been expanded to 100 percent and can be used for existing assets as well.

I know it sounds like Section 179 and bonus depreciation are the same, but they have two very important differences: there's no annual limit on bonus depreciation (unlike the $1 million limit under Section 179), and bonus depreciation is not limited to the profits (meaning it can create a net loss). These deductions can be tricky to maneuver, so talk to a pro.

While these bonuses help landlords, they also can help increase cash flows for indirect real estate investors. By increasing paper expenses to lower tax burdens, there's more money available to pass through to investors.

THE NEW 20 PERCENT RULE

The TCJA created a tax treasure for pass-through business owners, such as landlords set up as sole proprietorships, LLCs, and partnerships. Any profits earned through the rental properties get "passed through" to your personal income tax return. If your rental properties qualify as a business for tax purposes—and they almost always do when you actively participate in the business—the new tax law lets you deduct 20 percent of your net rental income from your taxable income. That can translate into huge tax savings, freeing up more money so you can beef up your investments or pay down some debt.

Be aware that this new twist is untested and the 20 percent deduction is reserved for *businesses*. If you own rental properties but aren't at all involved in the business of dealing with them, that wouldn't qualify for this deduction. But if you do participate in a meaningful way (which could mean anything from taking care of maintenance to screening tenants on your own), you probably will be able to take advantage of it. Talk with a qualified CPA before you decide to take the 20 percent; if you take it when you're not supposed to, the IRS will tack on a 10 percent penalty.

Pass-Through Math

Let's say you have one rental property, a single-family home. During the year, your tenants paid $30,000 in rent. Your expenses as a landlord (including mortgage interest, property taxes, and depreciation) came to $20,000. That means you earned $10,000 in profits ($30,000 – $20,000) from that property. That profit gets added to your other income, and you pay tax on your total income at the applicable tax rates.

But under TCJA, you can deduct 20 percent of that profit, or $2,000, from your total income (if your rental property qualifies as a business). Instead of paying tax on the full $10,000 of rental profits, you only have to pay tax on $8,000. Depending on your individual tax rate, that could save you hundreds, even thousands, of dollars on your tax bill.

The Rules

In order to qualify for that generous 20 percent deduction, you have to pass a few tests. First is the active participation test (you have to "work" at your rental properties). Next, there is an income test: your taxable income has to be less than $157,500 if you're single and less than $315,000 if you're married (filing jointly) to take the full deduction. It phases out entirely if you're taxable income hits $207,500 for singles or $415,000 for couples. In some cases, the deduction may still be available for landlords if they meet certain other qualifications; check with your accountant if that's your situation.

GET TO KNOW THESE TAX FORMS

Doing the Paperwork

If you're new to real estate investing (or investing in general), you'll need to familiarize yourself with some new tax forms whether you DIY taxes or hire a professional (which probably makes sense for the first year). The three main IRS forms you may be working with include Schedules E, B, and D, and all three are easily available on the IRS website (www.irs.gov).

Here's a quick breakdown of each form's purpose:

- Schedule E reports passive income from rental properties, partnerships, and trusts.
- Schedule B reports interest and dividend income.
- Schedule D reports capital gains and losses when you sell assets (like stocks, funds, or flip properties).

The forms can look complicated at first glance, but they're really pretty straightforward. If you're doing your own taxes, you'll need a higher level of DIY software than you probably used before; most of the basic versions don't come with all of these forms. The software will guide you through some questions, but they don't always cover everything, so it's good to know what should be on these forms.

SCHEDULE E:
SUPPLEMENTAL INCOME AND LOSS

When you invest in real property as a landlord, the IRS counts that as a passive activity (even if you're an active landlord), with all the income and expenses being reported on Schedule E.

However, if you're involved with short-term rentals (like Airbnb, for example), the IRS classifies that as a small business. In these cases, the income and loss would get reported on a different form (Schedule C) and you would definitely be eligible for the 20 percent deduction.

Easy Record Tracking

Landlords need to keep track of ongoing rental income and expenses along with anything that changes the cost basis of their property. The easiest way to do that: QuickBooks. It's simple to set up and use, and provides all the information your accountant (or your tax software) will need at the end of the year.

What Counts As Income?

When you're a landlord, you collect a lot of money, but not all of it counts as income for tax purposes. What counts is any kind of rent payment, no matter when you receive it (even an advance). Rental income also includes any extra money you receive from tenants to cover expenses (for example, they pay a portion of a utility bill). Other items that count as income include:

- Early cancellation fees (for tenants who don't stay for their whole lease)
- Monthly pet fees

- The value of services (like lawn care) performed by tenants in exchange for reduced rent

Any kind of tenant deposit (a security or pet deposit, for example) doesn't count as income, because it's not really your money; you have to give it back. The exception: if you keep a portion of the security deposit when the tenant vacates to cover damage to the property, that would count as income.

The Fourteen-Day Rule

If you rent your personal home for fourteen days or less during the year, that income does not have to be reported to the IRS. On the flip side, you don't get to deduct any expenses that you wouldn't normally deduct as a homeowner.

A Wealth of Deductible Expenses

Unlike the house you live in, practically every expense attached to your rental property counts as a deductible business expense for tax purposes. Expenses to deduct include:

- Mortgage interest
- Property taxes
- Insurance
- Homeowners association dues
- Advertising (to fill a vacancy)
- Utilities
- Repairs and maintenance
- Pest control
- Landscaping

- Trash pickup
- Depreciation

What doesn't count as an expense? Any major repairs or renovations you perform count as capital expenditures that get added to the cost basis of the property, effectively reducing your taxable income when you eventually sell.

Special Form for Depreciation

Depreciation gets special IRS attention, and requires Form 4562. To fill out this form (whether you're doing it with DIY software or providing info to your accountant), you'll need to know the basis of your rental property. The basis for depreciation is different than the overall basis because land does not get depreciated, and may change over time if you make improvements to the property.

To get started you'll need to know:

- The original purchase price of the property
- The list of closing costs (*most* closing costs get added to the basis)
- Land value, which you can find on the most recent property tax assessment paperwork
- Additions or improvements you made that will add value for more than one year (think replaced roof, not repainted rooms)
- The date the property was "placed in service," meaning made available for rent

The tax software will use that information to fill out Form 4562 and calculate depreciation expense for Schedule E.

THE "INVESTMENT" FORMS

When your real estate investing includes either house flipping (and you're not considered a "dealer" by the IRS) or indirect real estate investments (like stocks, REITs, and funds), the income will be reported on Schedules B and D.

For indirect investments, you'll get 1099 forms from your brokerage firm(s) in time to do your taxes. (These often end up being corrected, so you may want to wait for the final forms to file your taxes so you don't have to file an amended return.) Most brokerages will send one big combined form that contains:

- 1099-INT for interest income
- 1099-DIV for dividends and distributions
- 1099-B for investment sales

Your tax software will have fill-in forms that mimic the ones you get in the mail. Many versions also let you directly import your 1099s into the tax software.

Schedule B

If you earned at least $1,500 of interest or ordinary dividends during the year, you'll need to include Schedule B in your tax return. Real estate investors could earn interest from a variety of sources, including REITs, mortgage-backed securities, and crowdfunded debt, for example. Ordinary dividends could come from stocks, ETFs, mutual funds, or REITS. Both of these types of income get taxed at your regular income tax rate.

Some dividends, called qualified dividends, get special tax treatment. They're taxed at lower capital gains rates (which go as low as zero). The 1099 you receive will spell out whether dividends are ordinary or qualified.

Schedule D

Whenever you sell a capital asset for a gain or loss, that sale gets reported on Schedule D. The gains and losses are sorted based on timing: short-term for assets held for one year or less and long-term for assets held longer than one year. That timing matters because gains on short-term holdings are taxed at ordinary rates rather than the more favorable capital gains tax rates (0 percent, 15 percent, or 20 percent depending on your income).

Capital gains can be used to offset capital losses, and you only have to pay tax on your overall net capital gains. If you end up with a net capital loss, you can deduct up to $3,000 of it against your other income; the rest gets carried forward to the next year.

A Special Issue for Home Flippers

Many home flippers are considered "dealers" by the IRS, which considers them home-flipping businesses rather than investors. When you're first getting started, you may be able to avoid that classification, which is a much better tax situation. As an investor, you pay lower capital gains taxes on any property sale profits. As a dealer, you pay higher ordinary income tax rates *plus* self-employment taxes (Social Security and Medicare). If you do get stuck in this dealer category, you'll probably be eligible for the 20 percent deduction, so check with your tax preparer.

What lumps flippers into the dealer category? Earning most of your income from flipping and holding properties for short periods of time.

PASSIVE INCOME OFFSETS

The Passive/Active Balance

The IRS lumps income into three categories: portfolio, active, and passive. The portfolio class includes income from regular investments, like stocks, bonds, and mutual funds. Active income includes things such as salaries and wages, independent contractor earnings, and profits on a business you own and run. Passive income includes rental property income and limited partnership holdings, among other things.

The three income groups are treated differently for tax purposes, mainly when it comes to losses. Active losses can offset any other kind of income. Portfolio losses may offset other income but only partially. The rules are more complicated for passive activity losses—and that's where some real estate loopholes kick in.

RENTAL PROPERTY LOSSES ARE PASSIVE LOSSES

The IRS always considers rental property losses to be passive losses. Because of that, those losses can only be used to offset income from other passive activities, so you can't use them to reduce other taxable income (such as your job or stock dividends). That can be a big tax blow for most small landlords, who normally operate at a tax loss, especially in the beginning.

Cash and Profits Aren't the Same

Many new landlords collect enough rent to cover the mortgage, insurance, and other regular expenses, with some cash left over for themselves. And while some people consider that extra cash to be profits on their rental property, it's not. That's because not every cash outlay counts as an expense (like the principal portion of mortgage payments) and because of non-cash expenses.

When you're figuring out the profit or loss on your rental property, you'll have a big non-cash expense: depreciation. The deduction for that is normally enough to convert any rental property profits (if you're rental income has otherwise exceeded expenses) into losses for tax purposes.

Passive Offsets and Suspended Losses

Passive activity losses can only be used to offset passive activity profits. For example, if you have two rental properties and one earns profits while the other sustains losses, the losses can be used to reduce the profits. That will lower the tax bill on your overall rental property earnings. Those losses can also be used to offset income from other passive activities, like limited partnership or businesses you own but don't actively participate in (like a shop that you own but don't work at).

If you don't have enough passive income to absorb your passive losses, those losses get suspended until you can use them. That means you can use them to offset gains in future years, or reduce the capital gains when you eventually sell the property for a profit.

EXCEPTIONS TO THE PASSIVE LOSS RULES

Luckily, like most other IRS regulations, there are exceptions to the passive loss rules, and those can be very helpful for landlords. If you qualify for one of these exceptions (and most landlords can), you'll be able to deduct at least a portion of your rental property losses against all of your other income.

The two exceptions cover landlords who "actively participate" and real estate professionals. Both of those come with some strict IRS definitions, so make sure you really qualify (your CPA will be able to help if you're not sure) before you take the deduction.

The Active Participation Exception

If you "actively participate" with your rental properties, you may be able to deduct $25,000 of rental real estate losses against your other income. That provides a substantial tax benefit, somewhere in the neighborhood of $4,000 (depending on your loss amount and other income). Here, active participation means that you own at least 10 percent of the property and participate in meaningful management decisions (like approving tenants).

Know Your MAGI

MAGI is a tax calculation that doesn't show up anywhere on your tax return, but it's used to decide whether you qualify for special tax treatment. It includes a bunch of additions and subtractions (that will be done by your tax software), but basically it's your income after deductions for things like student loan interest and IRA contributions added back. For more information, visit www.irs.gov.

The catch: your modified adjusted gross income (MAGI) can't exceed $100,000 to get the full $25,000 deduction. At $100,000, the offset starts to phase out, and it disappears completely when MAGI hits $150,000.

Real Estate Professionals

If you qualify as a real estate professional under IRS rules, there's no limit on the amount of rental losses you can use to offset other income. As you'd expect, this exception comes with a much higher participation hurdle (you can find all the details in IRS Publication 527).

To get this special exemption from the passive loss rules, you (or your spouse) have to meet both of these requirements:

1. Spend more than half of your total working hours for the year in real estate activities
2. Spend more than 750 hours in real estate activities where you "materially participate" (which means you are regularly, continuously, and substantially involved)

Those sound similar, but there's a key difference: even if you spend 760 hours materially participating in real estate activities, for example, if you also spend 800 hours doing other work, you won't qualify.

WHAT HAPPENS WHEN YOU SELL

Going, Going, Gone

Whenever you sell an investment asset, you'll have either a gain or a loss. Either way, it gets reported on your tax return and helps determine your tax bill.

Capital gains income gets taxed at much lower rates (the highest is 20 percent) than other kinds of income. Most regular investments (like stocks, ETFs, mutual funds, and REITs) are always considered portfolio assets, and selling them will always result in capital gains (or losses), taxed at those beneficial rates. Still, if you can minimize or eliminate taxes, more of your money can go to work for you.

That's where direct real estate investments in rental properties can be especially handy, because they're entitled to some tax breaks that other assets aren't.

RENTAL PROPERTIES

When you're ready to sell your rental property, you may be in for a very large windfall. That could produce a substantial tax bill, unless you take some steps to reduce that tax burden. There are three main ways to do that with rental properties:

- Sell off some losing assets (like stocks that have plummeted) to offset the gain
- Structure a special deal called a 1031 exchange
- Turn the property into your primary residence for a couple of years before you sell

Without using any of these offsets, capital gains tax could make a huge dent in the amount of cash you get to keep.

1031 Exchange

If you want to sell a rental property but don't want to get out of the landlord game, you can take advantage of a special tax rule called the 1031 exchange (covered fully in the next section). In a nutshell, you basically sell your old property and buy a new one. Then, any capital gains you earned selling the old property get rolled up in the new property (sort of like trading in your car). Under the TCJA, *only* investment real estate qualifies for this special tax treatment.

This beneficial tax rule comes with a lot of technicalities and requirements, and it's important that you follow every one of them. To make sure your exchange goes smoothly and according to strict IRS guidelines, it's best to use a special professional called a Qualified Intermediary to facilitate the deal.

Transform It

If you turn your rental property into your own home for at least two years, you'll be eligible to shield up to $500,000 of capital gains (if you're married; $250,000 if you're single) from taxes. That's based on a rule designed to help homeowners, but the rule also allows landlords a nice little shelter.

Here's how it works: as long as you've owned the property for at least five years and lived there for at least two of the last five years, your property converts from an investment to a residence. The amount you get to exclude from capital gains tax depends on how long you've lived there.

For example, let's say you bought a rental house five years ago for $300,000 and rented it for three years. When your tenant moved out, you and your spouse moved in and stayed there for two years. You just sold the house for $400,000, a $100,000 capital gain. You can exclude two-fifths of that gain ($40,000) from taxes.

FLIP PROPERTIES

The whole point of the property-flipping business is to buy inexpensive "distressed" properties, fix them up, and sell them for a profit. When you're successful, those profits can be pretty big, and that means a huge tax bill.

As a home flipper, you'll want advantageous capital gains treatment for your property sales. But if it really has become routine for you, the IRS will consider you a dealer—and that puts you in an entirely different tax situation every time you sell a house.

As an Investor

Ideally, you'll be considered an investor, and your home-flip sales will be taxed using favorable capital gains tax rates. Unlike ordinary tax rates, capital gains taxes depend on how long you've held the asset. If you owned the house for one year or less, gains get taxed at ordinary rates (which range as high as 37 percent). If you've held the asset for more than a year, capital gains rates kick in (0 percent, 15 percent, or 20 percent depending on your overall income level).

Since many flips are quick, happening within just a few months, most home flippers end up paying tax at the ordinary rate. But that's still better than being considered a dealer. When your asset counts as an investment, it's not subject to self-employment (Medicare and Social Security) taxes of 15.3 percent, which comes on top of ordinary income taxes.

As a Dealer

If the IRS considers you a dealer, it means your house-flipping business counts as a business for tax purposes (even if you're just doing it as a side gig). All of your profits will be taxed at ordinary rates and be subject to self-employment taxes. Between the two, you could be paying as much as 52.3 percent (37 percent highest ordinary tax rate plus 15.3 percent self-employment tax) of your profits in taxes!

What would make the IRS consider you a dealer instead of an investor?

- You've flipped multiple homes during the year.
- Most of your work time is spent on flipping homes.
- A large percentage of your income is earned flipping houses.
- Your house-flipping business is active.

You may have noticed that those factors are vague; that's not an accident. The IRS hasn't published specific guidelines, so it's possible to fight dealer classification (especially if you have an experienced tax accountant). Remember, under the current tax law dealers may get to use the 20 percent deduction, which could result in a lower tax bill.

SECTION 1031 EXCHANGES

Trading Places

There's a section of the tax code that's like a holy grail for real estate investors. It's called the 1031 exchange (also known as a Starker exchange or a like-kind exchange), and it lets you continually buy and sell properties *without paying any capital gains taxes* as long as you do it properly. That's an enormous benefit, and one of the keys to building significant wealth with real estate.

Should You Do a 1031 Exchange?

Sometimes, it's not cost effective to do a 1031 exchange. In some cases, it makes more sense to do a straight sale, pay the capital gains tax, and move on to the next property at your own pace. Check with your CPA to see if a 1031 exchange makes sense for your situation.

Here's a simplified example of how it works: you buy a rental property for $100,000. A few years later, you sell it for $200,000 and use the proceeds to buy another property for $250,000. If your capital gains tax kicked in at 15 percent (the average, but the rate depends on your income level), you'd pay $30,000 in tax and have $170,000 to put toward the new building. With a 1031 exchange, you bypass the tax, save $30,000, and put the entire $200,000 toward your new purchase (the gain gets rolled into the new property value). That gives you $30,000 more equity, which probably qualifies you for a better interest rate on the mortgage, so you'll pay less interest over the life of the loan. And that's just the start of how the 1031 exchange helps build real estate empires. The key is to do it *exactly* right, and that calls for professional help.

THE RULES

The Tax Cut and Jobs Act changed a lot of rules in the tax code, many of them in favor of real estate investors specifically. The rules around 1031 exchanges fall into that category, because now *only* real estate qualifies for this kind of favored tax treatment (other business assets like planes, trucks, and manufacturing machinery used to be included).

To take advantage of this sweet tax deal, you have to follow the requirements perfectly (you do have to jump through some hoops). There are quite a few detailed rules to follow (whole books have been written about how to do this) but most of the time the incredible tax savings make it worthwhile.

No Cash for You

The number one rule of a 1031 exchange is: don't receive any money. Any actual cash you get during the deal will be taxed. What do you do with the money from the sale? That goes straight to a qualified intermediary who handles both ends of your property swap: the intermediary holds the proceeds from the sale and makes the payment for the new property.

If there's any cash left over (and sometimes there is), the intermediary turns it over at the end of 180 days. That money, called the "boot," gets taxed as proceeds from the property sale. In most cases, it will be treated as a capital gain, and taxed at your capital gains rate.

Like-Kind Guidelines

The basic premise of 1031 exchanges is the asset swap: you're essentially trading one asset for another. To qualify here, the assets have to be real estate and be "like-kind." Here are some examples of real estate assets that you could swap and benefit from the 1031 rules:

- Single-family rental property
- Multi-family rental property
- Apartment building
- Office building
- Strip mall
- Self-storage facility
- Hotel
- Raw land

You can also trade one property for multiple properties as long as the value is the same (for example, trading a $500,000 duplex for two $250,000 single-family rental properties).

There are some properties that don't qualify, such as your own home or your vacation home; it only counts for income-producing property (or property that's intended to produce income). Property specifically held for resale is also excluded, so this tax trick usually doesn't work for property flippers; it can work in some limited circumstances, so check with a professional to see if your situation qualifies.

The Timing

There are two key deadlines in the 1031 exchange process: identifying the swap property and closing the deal. Selling your property sets the timer on your 1031 exchange. Once your property has sold and the qualified intermediary has received the money, the forty-five-day clock starts on designating your intended replacement property. You have to identify the property in writing and hand that over to your qualified intermediary. If you're not 100 percent sure of what you want, you're allowed to designate up to three properties as long as you seal the deal on one of them by the closing deadline.

That second clock, the closing deadline, also starts when your original property is sold. You have 180 days from the day the sale closed to close on your new purchase.

The two clocks run at the same time. So if you don't designate your replacement property until day thirty-five, you'll only have 145 days left to close that deal.

THE QUALIFIED INTERMEDIARY

Using the wrong person as your QI can sink your 1031 exchange and make the entire deal taxable. Many 1031 novices mistakenly believe that as long as they don't touch the money, the IRS will bless the deal. But there are a lot of rules about who can and can't act as your QI.

Here's a list of who *cannot* act as your QI:

- A family member
- Your accountant (if he or she has done any non-exchange-related work for you over the past two years)
- Your lawyer (same rule as your accountant)
- Your real estate agent (same rule again)

It's in your best interests to hire a professional, experienced QI, especially if you're new to real estate investing. They can make sure you don't accidentally violate any of the cash or timing rules that could disqualify your deal.

OPPORTUNITY ZONE TAX BREAKS

Finding a Tax Heaven

Opportunity Zones offer the potential for enormous tax benefits—at least in theory. The rules for these investments are very new, and they haven't been tested yet, but they're likely to be extremely beneficial for real estate investors for decades to come. Basically, in exchange for some pretty astonishing tax incentives, investors pour money into financially or otherwise distressed areas (designated Opportunity Zones, or OZ) for at least ten years.

THE TAX BREAKS

All of the tax breaks available to OZ investors center around capital gains taxes, which are already subject to preferential treatment (mainly in the form of lower tax rates). This new investment vehicle offers two categories of tax breaks: one involves the money used to invest, and the other involves the OZ investment itself. All OZ investments have to be made through Qualified Opportunity Funds, companies which investors can set up or join.

To fully benefit from these tax incentives, there are a lot of rules to follow and hoops to jump through—do not attempt to navigate this without the help of a qualified tax professional (your nephew in business school won't cut it here).

Tax Deferral
The tax deferral advantage of OZ investing comes from capital assets you sell in order to have investment cash available. As long as

you invest those proceeds in an Opportunity Fund within 180 days, you can put off paying capital gains tax on your profits until either you sell (or exchange) your investment in the Opportunity Fund or December 31, 2026, whichever comes first.

For example, say you want to invest $50,000 in an OZ project, so you sell $50,000 worth of stock that you'd bought a few years earlier for $40,000. When you sell that stock, you have a $10,000 capital gain (the profit on the sale). Normally, you'd have to pay capital gains tax on that $10,000 right away. But if you put that $50,000 into an Opportunity Fund, you can delay paying that tax until 2026 (or when you sell off your fund share). That gives you more cash in hand right now, and more cash today is always a good thing.

Tax Reduction

If you hold your Opportunity Fund investment for at least five years (prior to December 31, 2026), you get a 10 percent discount on the capital gains tax bill for that deferred gain we covered earlier. And if you hold if for at least seven years, that discount grows to 15 percent.

Here's how that works: let's say your tax bill on that $10,000 gain would have been $2,000. If you keep the cash in the Opportunity Fund for at least five years, you'd get a $200 discount on that tax bill, and be required to pay only $1,800.

TAX-FREE GAINS

Because the whole point of OZ investing is to revitalize flagging economic areas, this could lead to unparalleled growth; the effect could potentially be much greater than would result from buying a building in an already thriving area. As the economy of an Opportunity Zone begins to improve and eventually flourish, property values could skyrocket—and that includes investments in Opportunity Funds.

To encourage continued investment presence in designated Opportunity Zones, the law includes a huge benefit for investors who stick around for the long haul. By holding Opportunity Fund investments for at least ten years, investors can escape *all* capital gains taxes on their investment. That's right, the law includes a permanent exclusion from capital gains taxes on the appreciation of OZ investments. And while there is a minimum holding period, there's no maximum holding period; gains can be taken fifteen or twenty years later (and those gains could be substantial) with no capital gains tax bite.

Here's how that works in comparison to a non-OZ investment: say you invested $50,000 in a Qualified Opportunity Fund, and you hold your investment for ten years. Over that time, the value increased by double, giving you a $50,000 capital gain when you sold your QOF investment. That $50,000 profit is all yours, tax-free. (You may still owe some capital gains tax on the money you used to invest, if that involved the deferred capital gains discussed earlier in this chapter.)

If instead of the QOF you'd invested that $50,000 in the stock market, you'd end up with less even if you gained more. Let's say (just for this example) that your $50,000 stock investment did brilliantly, and at the end of ten years was worth $110,000 for a $60,000 gain ($110,000 – $50,000). Come tax time, you'd owe (according to current tax law) $12,000 in capital gains tax at the 20 percent rate ($60,000 gain × 20 percent capital gains tax rate). That would leave you with a gain of $48,000; you'd have $2,000 less even though your money had earned $10,000 more than the hypothetical QOF investment.

REAL ESTATE IN RETIREMENT ACCOUNTS

Save Some for Later

Real estate makes a good long-term investment, and that makes it a perfect holding for retirement accounts. Keeping real estate locked away for retirement helps investors ignore the temporary economic ups and downs that can affect property values and income streams.

With a wide range of investment types to choose from, you can have an entire real estate portfolio among your retirement assets. And with self-directed IRAs, your real estate investment options are virtually unlimited.

TWO KINDS OF IRAS

Individual retirement accounts, or IRAs, are self-directed, tax-advantaged accounts where you can stash money that you'll need when you eventually retire. Compared to an employer-sponsored retirement plan such as a 401(k), an IRA gives you more control over what you invest in, what fees you're willing to pay, and which institution will house your account. This gives you much more flexibility and freedom, along with a much broader range of investment options.

IRAs come in two main types, traditional and Roth, and they have many differences. Either style can be used for a self-directed IRA (which gives you the most autonomy over investment options). To contribute to either kind, though, you have to have *earned* income (from a job or a business, for example)—investment and rental income don't count.

IRA Balances Are Growing

According to Fidelity Investments, the average IRA balance (as of September 30, 2018) rose to $111,000. That comes along with a 25 percent increase in the number of IRA millionaires.

Traditional

Traditional IRAs give you a current tax break along with tax-deferred growth on your investments. Contributions to an IRA get subtracted from your taxable income, lowering your income tax bill for the year. As the money in your IRA grows, you get to sidestep paying taxes on the earnings (unlike a regular investment account where you pay tax on the earnings every year). That helps your money grow even faster, letting you build up a bigger nest egg than you would if you were constantly losing a big chunk of it to the IRS. When you eventually begin taking withdrawals after age fifty-nine-and-a-half, you'll pay tax on whatever amount you pull out every year.

Those tax benefits come with some pretty strict rules. For one thing, if you take any of that money out before you turn fifty-nine-and-a-half (unless it's for an allowable reason), you'll pay some hefty tax penalties on top of the immediate income tax bite. On the flip side, you *have to* start taking required minimum distributions (RMDs) once you turn age seventy-and-a-half, whether or not you want to. To learn more about the ins and outs of IRAs, visit www.irs.gov.

Roth

Roth IRAs have several distinct advantages over traditional IRAs and a couple of potential drawbacks. On the downside, you don't get a current tax deduction for a contribution to a Roth IRA, and your income level may limit your allowable contributions (visit www.irs.gov for details on this). Everything else about Roth IRAs is a plus:

- You can take out any money you contributed at any time with no tax issue.
- You don't have to pay tax on earnings as your money grows.
- As long as you wait five years *and* until you're at least age fifty-nine-and-a-half, you can withdraw earnings *tax-free*.
- You never have to take money out if you don't want to.
- You can leave the money to heirs tax-free (though they will have to take RMDs).

REGULAR VERSUS SELF-DIRECTED

Though the contribution and taxation rules are the same for regular and self-directed IRAs, the types of investments they can hold are very different. The options with regular IRAs are much more limited, usually controlled by whichever financial institution (usually a bank or brokerage firm) houses the account.

Typically, in a regular IRA you can invest in "regular" things, like CDs (certificates of deposit), stocks, bonds, mutual funds and ETFs, and publicly traded REITs. Plus, within those regular investment categories, you may be limited by which funds or fund types are available. That still gives you a lot of options, but not enough for diehard real estate investors.

That's where self-directed IRAs come in. Here, you can invest in almost anything. In fact, the list of things you can't invest in is much shorter than what you can invest in. That no-go list includes insurance instruments or collectibles, which leaves virtually any kind of real estate investment on the okay list. A self-directed IRA can be used for:

- Rental properties
- House flipping
- Crowdfunded real estate
- Real estate limited partnerships
- Private and unlisted REITs
- Interval funds

Opportunity Funds

To use your IRA for these types of investments, you'll have to work with a more specialized custodian. It's also smart to work with an experienced financial advisor to choose an appropriate and reputable custodian, get your account set up, and create a well-diversified investment plan (your retirement savings should not include only one asset class).

Beware of Prohibited Transactions

In order to maintain the favorable tax status of your IRA, stay away from transactions prohibited by the IRS. These taboo transactions include taking personal loans against your account and self-dealing (such as buying a rental property and renting it to your child).

ESTIMATED TAXES—MAKING PAYMENTS

Your Best Guess

When you get a regular paycheck, your employer sends a portion of your earnings straight to the IRS to cover your federal and state income taxes, Social Security, and Medicare. When you're earning money from real estate investing, that doesn't happen automatically. Since you're earning income, you will have to pay taxes. And since no one is taking care of that for you, you have to handle those payments yourself.

What happens if you don't make payments during the year, and instead just wait until you file your tax return and pay it all then? Penalties and interest. And that will seriously eat into your profits and your savings.

COMING UP WITH THE ESTIMATE

The IRS gets very picky about estimated tax payments, which are required if you'll end up owing at least $1,000 in taxes for the year. Not only do you have to pay on time, your payments have to be big enough. So even if you make every payment on time, if the IRS thinks you underpaid, they'll still hit you with penalties and interest (but only on the underpayment amount).

That's why you want to come up with a realistic estimate. You don't want to underpay and leave yourself open to an even bigger tax hit. But you also don't want to overpay and let the IRS hold on to your money interest-free for most of the year.

Figure Out Your Taxable Income

To come up with a solid estimate, you'll need to figure out how much taxable income you *expect* to earn over the whole year. This means you have to include every possible source of income, whether it's from investments, rental properties, Social Security, or a regular job. Even though money you earn at a regular job already has tax taken out, you still need to include it because it plays a part in determining your tax rates.

If you're not sure how much income you can expect—common for new investors—there are a few things you can do to help you come up with a reasonable estimate:

- Talk to your accountant.
- Look at past dividend payouts on stocks, funds, and REITs you hold.
- Figure out your projected profit on rental properties by subtracting the known expenses for the year from the total rent.
- Figure out potential profits on a flip house by subtracting the cost of the property plus improvements from comparable home sales.
- For hard-to-track investments (like unlisted REITs or interval funds), call the issuer and ask for an estimate.

After the first year, this will be much easier because you'll have a better idea of investment income production.

Figure Out the Estimated Tax

Once you have a handle on your expected taxable income for the year, you'll need to calculate the tax. If you used tax prep software last year, it has the forms you need: Form 1040-ES and payment vouchers. You just have to input your expected income and the software will figure out your estimated tax payments. You can also get the forms, vouchers, and worksheets you need on the IRS website (www.irs.gov).

You'll have three categories of taxes:

1. Ordinary income tax on short-term capital gains, house-flipping income (if you're a dealer), rental income, interest and dividend income from investments, and any job-type income (whether it's a regular job, side gig, or contract work)
2. Capital gains tax on long-term capital gains (for investment assets sold during the year) and qualified dividends
3. Self-employment tax on any house-flipping income (if you're a dealer) or contract work

Once you come up with your estimated tax total, you'll divide that number by four. You'll send in four equal payments on estimated tax payment dates: April 15, June 15, September 15, and January 15.

Remember State Taxes

If you have to pay estimated income taxes to the IRS, you'll probably need to make estimated state income taxes payments also. Every state has its own rules for this, so check with your state's taxing authority (easily found online) to find out what you'll need to do.

A lot of people get anxious when they're doing this for the first time (and some people every time) because they're afraid they'll get it very wrong. If you're worried about that, there's an easy fix called the "safe harbor" requirement: pay at least what you paid last year (or 110 percent of last year's total tax bill if your taxable income was more than $150,000). That way, no matter how much money you end up owing (even if it's a lot), the IRS won't charge any penalties.

INDEX

ABOUT THE AUTHOR

Michele Cagan is a CPA, author, and financial mentor. With more than twenty years of experience, she offers unique insights into personal financial planning, from breaking out of debt and minimizing taxes to maximizing income and building wealth. Michele has written numerous articles and books about personal finance, investing, and accounting, including *The Infographic Guide to Personal Finance*, *Investing 101*, *Stock Market 101*, and *Financial Words You Should Know*. In addition to her financial know-how, Michele has a not-so-secret love of painting, Star Wars, and chocolate. She lives in Maryland with her son, dogs, cats, and koi. Get more financial guidance from Michele by visiting SingleMomCPA.com.

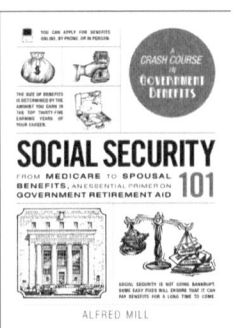

A CRASH COURSE IN
EVERYTHING YOU NEED TO KNOW!

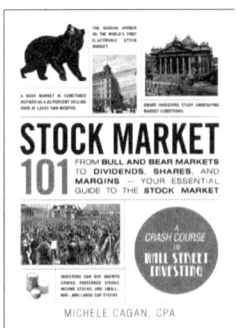